ANCIENT JUDICIAL SYSTEM OF INDIA

ANCIENT JUDICIAL SYSTEM OF INDIA

DR. GOKULESH SHARMA
Judge, Civil Court, Lucknow

DEEP & DEEP PUBLICATIONS PVT. LTD.
F-159, Rajouri Garden, New Delhi-110027

ANCIENT JUDICIAL SYSTEM OF INDIA

ISBN 978-81-8450-049-3

Typeset by ASHISH TECHNOGRAPHICS,
3190, Mohindra Park, Shakur Basti, Delhi-110034.

Printed in India at NEW ELEGANT PRINTERS,
A-49/1, Maya Puri, Phase-I, New Delhi-110064.

Published by DEEP & DEEP PUBLICATIONS PVT. LTD.
F-159, Rajouri Garden, New Delhi-110027.
Phones: 25435369, 25440916
E-mail: ddpbooks@yahoo.co.in • ddpubs@gmail.com
Showroom:
2/13, Ansari Road, Daryaganj, New Delhi-110002 • Telefax: 23245122

Dedicated to

My elder Brother Pandit Sunder Lal Sharma, who tried to bring amalgamation of Ancient India Culture and Tradition with the Modern Legal System

Contents

Preface

Indian culture is still the best in the world. Number of residents of U.S.A. and other European countries are sincerely but slowly, regularly but steadily, adopting our culture and heritage. In view of fast developing love, affection and attachment to our culture, by foreigners, it is necessarily felt that there should be complete book, which deals with our purely Indian culture, old and Ancient Judicial system. The purpose of this book is clear. It is meant to show to foreigners that not only our culture, tradition and philosophy was superior, but also our judicial system was also matchless. It was the gap of time and lack of connection between Eastern and Western culture, which created ignorance. Now it is not the position, both foreign and west is trying to consolidate themselves into joint platform. Earlier West was said to be best and best thought themselves to be best but now they have understood themselves. They cannot survive without each other. They are complimentary to each other. Now it is essential to fill up the gap. The present book shall not only fill up the Gap of Eastern thoughts to Western Ideas. It shall be now possible to study complete Ancient Judicial system through this book. All attempts have been made to consolidate entire Ancient system into one concise book. The detailed study of eastern judicial system would take lacs of pages. Hence, precise and valuable brief has been written completely of entire Ancient Judicial System.

The present book is divided into two major parts—First is unwritten of Smtri period and Second is of Mahabharat epic period. Both these periods are roughly contemporary, but for our purposes, we have divided it into two major aspects.

The first part of the book deals with the unwritten and Smrti period. It is oldest unavailable thought. The authencity of these kinds of thoughts is made from various available Smrti and old written essays by western poets, kings or other writers.

The second part deals with the epic age. The valuable contribution of the Mahabharata, Bhagwata Gita is explicitly clear. But relevant references have been taken up for study here. Roughly it can be said that all attempts have been made to collect the entire clear cut picture of Ancient and old Indian Judicial system.

Another part of the book consists of two divisions: first administration and second judicial. First part consist of six chapters and second part consist of seven chapters. There are totally thirteen chapters. The detail of first part belongs to Smrti and unwritten period. This part is out of the oldest part. Several researches have been made for this period. Roughly I have collected all. The contribution of Professor R.S. Sharma and Kalkan is very high and unforgettable. The contribution of other writers can also not be ignored. Relevant references of other writers have been made at relevant places.

The four chapters in the beginning relate to ancient Indian political concepts and the functioning of the state and its administration. The subsequent four chapters dealing with vyavahara, courts, crime and punishment and orders are an effort to investigate the basic legal concepts during the period as also the mode and methods for the administration of justice. Readers will appreciate that this legal framework operated during the age when religious and secular ideas were still intermingled with each other and they both influenced the working of the state and its administration. Besides, belief in many superstitious ideas had also not a small role in the actual administration of justice. It is hoped that the readers will find the study somewhat useful and appreciate the working of the study of the legal system in the context of the times when it prevailed.

The last three chapters deal with property laws, varna legislations and laws of family. The study of these vital socio-economic aspects in ancient India is neither exhaustive nor is it expected that the readers will find themselves in agreement with all the conclusions.

The socio-economic aspects of ancient India ,have not lost their relevance even today when the country is set on the road to modernization. Attrocities on harijans, violent caste conflicts, dowry deaths and widespread exploitation and oppression of women have assumed serious proportions even after more than five decades of independence. All thinking persons are rightly over this matter and are keen to find ways and means to contain and eliminate the forces which undermine national integrity and civilized life. It is always better to properly diagnose the disease and find out its genesis in order to cure it completely. It is hoped that the present study may be helpful, even though on a limited scale, to analyze and understand the ancient Indian background of these fissiparous ailments in the body politic of present day Indian Judicial system.

I think the book as a whole shall contribute as a complete study of Ancient Indian Judicial system. The book has been written in fool proof manner. If any mistake is discovered or found, I am rendering all due apologises for the same in advance. I require suggestions for reform in future about the book. I shall heartedly welcome them.

The book is dedicated to my late elder brother Shri Sunderlal Sharma who was a ideal saint and *yogi* in the true sense and inspired me to prosecute everything for the causes of our own culture and tradition.

In last, I shall be able to say that the book shall be useful to all who are interested to be true Indian in cultural sense. It is also useful for those also who want to know about Indian culture and tradition.

Lucknow DR. GOKULESH SHARMA

PART I

Chapter

1

Origin of State

In ancient India monarchy was accepted form of government though side by side we get the example of republics also. Professor Macdonell rightly says, "It is quite clear that the normal, though not universal form of government in early India was by kings, as might be expected in view of the fact that the Aryan Indians were invaders in a hostile territory; a situation which as in the case of the Aryan invaders of Greece and of the German invaders of England, resulted almost necessarily in strengthening the monarchial element of the constitution."[1] But the smrti-writters mention the monarchic form of government only. The office of the king stood for the state also. How did this state come into being? It is question that has attracted the attention of the western as well as oriental political thinkers, and they speculated on several theories to explain this phenomenon. Our ancient Indian political thinkers also did not lag behind and they did devoted some attention to this matter, although their speculations were not elaborated with the same minuteness of detail as those of some of the European theorists. They would not perhaps be entirely devoid of

1. Macdonnel, Vedic Index, Vol. III, p. 210.

interests for the students of political philosophy.[2] In other words, ancient Indian thinkers also enquired about the origin of government or the origin of kingship.

One of the several theories propounded by political thinkers regarding the origin of the state is the divine theory. It implies that the state is the creation of god and therefore it is a divine institution. Closely connected with this theory is the theory of divine right, which enunciates that the king enjoys unlimited right and there is nobody on this earth who can delimit his powers. Disobedience should lead to death. In other words, it can be stated that both the theories advocated the principle of passive submission to the king on the part of the subjects.

Certain smrti-writers give the impression that the theory of divine origin was known to them. The antiquity of this theory in ancient India cannot be easily established. Spellman is of the opinion that during the early Vedic period the king did not claim divine descent. He further states that it is only in the later period descent. He further states that it is only in the later period that the idea of divine origin got prominence.[3] But U.N. Ghoshal finds some traces of the divinity of king during the Rgvedic period also. He points out that the honorific epithet Rajan is repeatedly applied to the great gods, Indra, Mitra, Varuna, Brhaspati, Soma and Yama as well as to a number of deities. But at the same time he admits that the Rgvedic king never claimed divine descent. Neither his office nor his person could ever be regarded as divine.[4]

The idea of divinity is conspicuously missing in the Dharmasutras and Arthasastra and it seems that due to Buddhistic influence no divine sanction is granted to the king. It is in the metrical smrtis that the theory is expounded in full. Among the metrical smrti-writers Manu, Narada and Katyayana devote some verses to the treatment of the theory. Manu says that when confusion prevailed god created the

---

2. P.N. Benerjee, Public Administration in Ancient India, p. 34.
3. Spellman, Political Theory of Ancient India, p. 37.
4. U.N. Ghoshal, IHQ, Vol. XX, 1994, p. 39.

king.[5] Thus we find that in the opinion of Manu kingship was created not be mortal. There are several verses in Santi Parva regarding the divine creation of kingship.[6]

Our smrti-writers compare the king with different deities as one who discharges multifarious duties. Manu states that in order to perform his protective duties properly the king takes the attributes of Indra, Vayu, Yama, Sun, Agni, Varuna, Moom and the lord of wealth (Kuber). Narada also states that the king is the incarnation of different deities. As the king possesses enormous powers he appears to have the aspects of five different deities—Agni, Indra, Soma, Yama and the Kubera.[7] Katyayana adds that the chief of gods (Indra), coming down from heaven stands before the people in the form of king, but this lawgiver also asks the king to acts in such a manner that he attains the position of Indra.[8] Therefore Katyayana's idea does not take the divinity of the king for granted. In his opinion the king has also to earn and deserve it. Every king cannot attain the position of Indra, except virtuous kings. Katyayana's idea is found in some other texts also. Santi Parva states that it is Indra who is crowned in the person of the king.[9]

Certain Puranas also contain similar ideas regarding king's divinity. The Agni Purana states that the king assumes the functions of eight deities. He acts as Bhaskara (sun) because it is difficult to gaze at him, and he acts as moon for his presence gladdens the people. He sweeps the world with spies, punishes the evil-doers and burns them, and so is compared with Samira, Manu Vaivasvata and Pavaka (fire) respectively. Like Kubera (god of wealth) and Varuna (god of water) he makes gifts to the brahmannasans showers wealth on the people. He sustains the people like Prthvi and finally in the capacity of Hari protects his subjects through the three

5. Manu, VII, 3.
6. SP, 59, 127, 128, 133, 134, 135.
7. Nar. XVIII, 26.
8. Kat. 8.
9. Sp, 67, 4.

types of energies.[10] Besides Agni Purana, Matsya,[11] Padma,[12] and Markandeya[13] Puranas refer to the idea of the functional resemblance between the king and some of the deities. All these imply that in several texts the idea of divinity was introduced to enumerate the functions of the king. Spellman calls it a 'functional divinity'.[14]

Certain epigraphic sources also confirm that this concept of functional divinity existed in India during the period of our law-givers. In one of the Asokan inscriptions it is found that the king used the title of 'Devanam-priya'.[15] During the Gupta period kings were compared with the different deities. In the Mathura stone-inscriptions Samudra Gupta is considered as equal to the gods Dhanada, Varuna, Indra and Antaka; the last thought to be the very axe of the god of Kritanta.[16] Not only in India but in other countries too kings were deified. Alexander the Great and Julius Caesar had their decent traced to gods and goddesses. Alexander was deified during the lifetime, in 344 BC by the Greek world and Caesar's image was carried among those of immortal gods.[17] Maine remarks, "Heroic Kingship depended partly on divinely given prerogative, and partly on the possession of super eminent strength, courage and wisdom."[18]

The comparison of the king with the different deities is intended to emphasize his superior position in society. Manu argues that a king is made of the particles of the lords of the gods, and therefore he surpasses all the created beings in luster.[19] Furthermore, he repeats that like the sun, the king burns eyes and hearts, and it is very difficult for a person to gaze at him.[20] Manu emphatically justifies the superior

10. Agni, P., pp. 226, 17-20.
11. Matsya, P., Ch. 22.
12. Padma, P., pp. 1, 30, 45 ff.
13. Mark, P., pp. 27, 21 ff.
14. Spellman, Political Theory of Ancient India, p. 30.
15. V.A. Smith, Ashoka, p. 165 (fn. 2. Edict. VIII).
16. CII, Vol. III, No. 60, p. 257.
17. P.V. Kane, HDS. Vol. III, p. 29.
18. Maine, Ancient Law, p. 9.
19. Manu, VII, 5.
20. *Ibid.*, VII, 6.

position of the king. He states that even an infant king must not be despised for he is a great deity in human form.[21] The same idea is echoed by Narada.

Narada states that one must not treat him with contempt. And particularly must not scold him; obedience should be rendered; for to disobey him would bring instantaneous death.[22]

The texts quoted above are difficult to interpret. Some authorities conclude that the twin theory of divine origin and divine right was enunciated by our smrti-writers while others hold that such a theory was completely absent during that period. U.N. Ghoshal says that we find in them a closest approach to the western theory of divine right.[23] Bhandarkar opines that the theory of divine origin was maintained in India though it was never pushed to any absurd limit.[24] Kane also agrees with Bhandarkar and says that the idea of divine nature of the king dies not mean that ancient Hindu political thinkers were in favour of giving unlimited powers to the king.[25]

Certain western scholars also state that the theory of divine origin prevailed in ancient India. Spellman asserts, "In ancient India, therefore, the king in theory at least, went through the complete catalogue of claims to divinity.[26] To allege that the king was neither believed nor claimed to be divine is nonsense." In order to justify his views he quotes some other authorities in whose opinion divinity of the king had great spell over the minds of the Indian people. Vaidya remarks that Indians came to look upon their king's person as inviolable and his order as the word of god, and this attitude dominated the minds of the people so completely that they because slavish in their allegiance to him and their attachment to his person became proverbial and continues to be so sown to this day.[27] The idea of divinity had engulfed

21. *Ibid.*, VII, 8.
22. Nar. XVIII, 32.
23. U.N. Ghoshal, A History of Indian, Political Thought, p. 229.
24. D.R. Bhandarkar, Some Aspects of Ancient Kindu Polity, p. 142.
25. P.V. Kane, HDS, Vol. III, pp. 25-26.
26. Spellman, Political Theory of Ancient India, p. 38.
27. Vaidya, quoted by Spellman, Political Theory of Ancient India, p. 40.

the minds of the Indians so much that Professor Basham remarks laconically. "Divinity was cheap in ancient India."[28] Hocart while quoting Manu also justifies his contention that divine kingship was clearly a feature of early Indian thought.[29]

But some writers have completely rejected the prevalence of the idea of divinity in ancient India. Rejecting this idea Panikkar says: "By no stretch of imagination can it be interpreted to mean that the king in his own person was Indra, Yama, Dharma. He was to possess the qualities of these three."[30] He further tolds that the functions of the king, and not the king himself, are usually equated with gods. Rejecting the idea of the divinity of Indian kings Drekmeir says, "As a consequence of the ritual the ruler became god like, but this was not meant to imply that he became a god or even that his office necessarily received divine sanction." He further enjoins, "The word he further enjoins", The word 'deva' is often translated by western scholars as 'god'. Deva is used, however, to connote moral superiority rather than omnipotent divinity in the judeo-Christian sense."[31] Sen also voices the same opinion when he says that divinity belongs rather to the high office than the person of the king.[32] Altekar seems to agree with Sen when he says, "Hindu writers have thus advocated the divinity, not of the person of the king but of his office, because of the resemblance between his functions and those of some deities.[33] N.C. Bandoadhayaya totally rejects the divine theory by saying that the king could neither claim divinity not had he any prerogative.[34] Dikshitar does not believe that the divine theory enunciated by the smrti-writers had any thing to do with the actuality. His idea

28. A.L. Basham, The Wonder that was India, p. 86.
29. Hocart, quoted by E. Burk, The Divine Right of Persian Kings, JIH, Vol. XLV, Part II, 1917.
30. Panikkar, Origin and Evolution of Kingship, p. 35.
31. Drekmeir, Kingship and Community in Early India, p. 251.
32. A.K. Sen, Studies on Hindu Political Thought, p. 57.
33. A.S. Altekar, State and Government in Ancient India, p. 61.
34. N.C. Bandopadhyaya, quoted by Spellman, Political Theory of Ancient India, p. 26.

regarding the divine theory is: "If once he had been consecrated to the exalted place of kingship, which meant presidentship over the destinies of millions of his subjects, he should be regarded by the public with a certain amount of veneration and awe. Such veneration was due to the place he occupied and not to the person or the individual king whoever he might be." In this connection he further says that any and every king was not treated as a god from heaven on earth fit to be an 'object of worship'. Kings who followed the righteous path of administration were entitled to some consideration, and it is no wonder that such kings were looked upon with the certain amount of veneration. This has nothing to do with the divine theory of kings as promulgated in some of our law-books.[35] P.N. Banerjee also confirms that kingship in India was a political office, and not the sphere of power of a fortunate individual.[36]

Whatever may be the ideas of the different authorities regarding the divine origin in ancient India it would not be proper to reject completely the existence of this concept during the time of our smrti-writer. Some kind of divine sanction was granted to the authority of the king. But at the same time it should be noted that the western concept of the divine right theory of the king is non-existent.

Why did smrti-writers grant divinity to the king? It seems that the contemporary situation of the country made it essential to create some king of divine halo around him so that the subjects would render passive obedience to him.

Apart from this there seems to be another contributory factor. Like the western political thinkers our smrti-writers too used this theory to serve their own purpose or to suit their own point of view. All were staunch advocate to the monarchic form of government and Brahmanism. It seems that in order to strengthen their own point of view they enunciated the theory of the divine origin of kingship. The doctrine of the king's divine personality was deliberately

35. V.R. Dikshitar, Gupta Polity, pp. 113-14.
36. Banerjee, Public Administration in India, p. 72.

introduced by the canonical authors with the object of strengthening the principle of authority.[37] Manu was a staunch advocate of the absolute monarchy and therefore he utilized the idea of divinity of king to strengthen his own view. Manusmrti is also known as the code of Sumati and it was written to support a usurper (Pusyamitra). The author had to teach that the king was not to be treated lightly.[37a] Narada also used this theory to justify his view regarding the absolute rule of a king. But Katyayana makes a departure. He states that kings who abide by the duties peculiar themselves are elevated to the position of Indra; but those kings whose actions go astray from the path of Dharma have to reside in the Avici (hell) after death.[38]

While examining the divine theory we should keep in mind the fact that this did not emerge suddenly during the smrti period but had its roots even in the Vedic texts smrti treatment of this aspect of kingship is significant because the smrtis have introduced a consistency in the theory that the king had a supernatural and divine character. Some have explained that this was as a reaction the intrusion of foreigners like the Greeks, Sythians and the Kusansa during the first century BC.[39]

Much reliance however cannot be placed on the external factor playing a decisive role in this matter. B.G. Gokhale also states other causes contributing to the rise and acceptance of divine theories.[40] According to him the tribal state was during his period being transformed into a regional state and an ever-expanding state. This process rendered difficult the existence of popular assemblies like the sabha and samiti which ultimately disappeared leading to 'an enormous increase in the concentration of power of the monarchies, the exercise of which was rendered difficult because of the backwardness of communication and the existence of numerous regional political society.' Under these

---

37. U.N. Ghoshal, A History of Indian Political Thought, p. 80.
37a. K.P. Jayaswal, Manu and Yajnavalkya, pp. 98-99.
38. Kat. 8.
39. B.G. Gokhale, Samudra Gupta, p. 61.
40. *Ibid.*, pp. 62-63.

circumstances kingship felt the need for acquiring a theological sanction and tradition. Gokhale has correctly pointed to another and more fundamental cause of the transformation of Indian society from the tribal to the nation stage. So long as the society was essentially tribal, ties and loyalty could be effective. With the society being transformed into multitribal, multiracial and multicultural, reliance could not be placed in securing obedience to king's commands on the basis of tribal loyalties. Therefore, divinity of kingship was one means of supplanting the old tribal tie. Another explanation is related to the conflict between two forms of governments during the period, Gokhale's divine theory provided the theological justification for the destruction of the oligarchic republics as also their easy transition to monarchies.

Gokhale's explanation for the rising importance of the divine theory of kingship is correctly based on the changing character and role of the state. But it fails to take onto account another important factor, i.e. the economic factor. The period of smrtis, i.e. the 4th century BC to the 6th century AD, is also a period of fundamental economic changes in Indian society. The rise and strengthening of private property, emergence of feudal relationships and of conflicting classes like owners of land and cattle on the one hand and sharecroppers, ploughmen and cowherds, etc. on the other, all point to the weakening and undermining of the tribal ties and loyalties and growing conflict between persons and classes, between owners of property and actual tillers. This conflict probably has been the most important factor responsible for the growing emphasis in Manu and other smrtis on *danda* which alone could keep such a conflict-ridden society alive. The divine theory made the coercive powers of *danda* and the king supreme and facilitated their effective roles in preventing the class and caste-ridden society from destruction due to its internal stresses and strains.

Chapter

2

Kingship

During the vedic period the office of the king was elective, but gradually it became hereditary. In the law books we do not get any description of the coronation ceremony. In the Dharmasutras we find stray reference to this subject. Vasistha declares that after the coronation of a new king the capital grows again.[1] This only shows that kings were formally crowned. The Gupta inscriptions prove and show.[2] It seems that the system of coronation was so well established that our smrti-writers did not bother to give much attention to it.

QUALITIES OF THE KING

In ancient India the king was the pivot around whom the whole administrative machinery revolved. Therefore, the smrti-writers take much pain to state the qualities, which a king must possess. They consider him to be a superman. He should possess such qualities as would exalt his position in society. On account of the increases complexities of

1. Vas, Dh. S. II 50.
2. CII Vol. III, No. 1, pp. 11-12.

administration the law-givers preferred to vest the ruling power in the hands of such a person as would control and keep in obedience the subjects.

First, great emphasis is laid on the education of the king. The smrti-writers recommended that the king should be endowed with the study of the Sastras.[3] They also prescribe purity in acts and speech on his part. In other words, they enjoin truthfulness in speech; the king should be devoted to truth and dharma.[4]

Manu asks the king to acquire the knowledge of the three Vedas. The king is also advised to learn the science of government, science of dialectics and acquire the knowledge of the supreme soul as well as of trade and business.[5]

Further Manu suggests that the king should not do anything in haste but should thing carefully. He should possess good common sense, and should know the respective values of virtue, pleasure and wealth.[6]

Modesty is another virtue the importance of which is stressed by Manu strongly. He advises the king to learn modesty from the aged and learned brahmans as it prevents his destruction. Manu shows that immodesty leads to the destruction of the king together with the kingdom but modesty helps in regaining the lost kingdom.[7] Katyayana also asks the king to cultivate humility.[8]

Certain smrti-writers recommend the outward decoration of the king. The king is advised to get himself bedecked with jewels. Obviously emphasis over impressive outward appearance was laid to lend glory to the position of the king and at the same time to distinguish him from the common people. The smrtikars add that the king should be pleasing in appearance as well as should be a man of happy disposition.[9]

---

3. Kat. 1-2.
4. Gaut, Dh. S. XI 2; Manu VII, 26; Kat. 1-2.
5. Manu, VII , 43 Yaj. I. 311-14; Kat. 1-2.
6. Manu, VII, 31.
7. *Ibid.*, VII. 39-40.
8. Kat. 1-2.
9. Visnu, III. 86, 89-90; Kat. 1-2.

Intelligence is another quality, which should be present in a ruler according to Manu, Yajnavalkya and Narada.[10] The king should be also self-sacrificing. He should be always ready to sacrifice everything for the good of the people, and so Manu suggests that he should not go by his own likes and dislikes.[11]

A king must possess enthusiasm to enable him to execute the different plans of government.[12]

As the fountainhead of justice he should possess the sense of impartiality otherwise he will not be able to discharge his judicial duties properly. Our smrti-writers suggest that the king should inflict punishment justly.[13]

Some of these qualities are also enumerated in the Santi Pavra. Like good conduct, self-control, humility, righteousness, beauty, liberality, etc. It is also suggested that the king should dress himself gorgeously.[14] Epigraphic sources indicate that at least some kings did possess mental as well as physical qualities. Samudra Gupta possessed the various qualities prescribed by the law-givers.[15]

The smrti-writers display a deep insight into human nature. They were conscious of the fact that the king might fall a prey to the different vices which would hinder his work. Therefore, they ask the king to control his senses, for he alone who has conquered his own senses can keep his subjects in obedience.[16] Manu enumerated the vices in much detail. He states; "Let him carefully shun the ten vices, springing from love of pleasure, and the eight proceedings from wrath, which all end in misery." The vices which arise from love of pleasure are hunting, gambling, sleeping during day, curiosity, excessive indulgence in sex, drunkenness, an inordinate love for dancing, singing and music, and unless travel. Furthermore tale-bearing, violence, treachery, envy,

10. Manu, VII, 140; Yaj. I 309-11; XVIII.19.
11. Manu, VIII, 133.
12. Yaj. I. 309-11.
13. Manu, VII, 26 Br. I Kat. 1-2.
14. Sp, X 19; LVII 22.
15. CII, Vol. III, No. I, pp. 12-15.
16. Manu, VII, 244, Sp. LVII. 22.

slandering, seizure of property, reviling and assault are some of the vices which arise from wrath. Manu advises the king not only to avoid and overcome all these vices but also greediness which all wise men declare to be the root of both these sets of vices.[17]

Unlike Manu Yajnavalkya does not enumerate separately the vices of the king, but while discussing the qualities he advises the king to control his senses and to get rid of some of these vices. He suggests that the king should be neither lowly nor harsh. He should get rid of bad habits and act as the 'guardian of his weak points'.[18] Katyayana advises the king to be free from haughtiness, harassment of subjects, wickedness, rashness, irascibility, etc.[19] Visnu, like other smrti-writer, forbids the king to take delight in hunting, dice-playing, sex, drinking, defamation and flattery.

It seems that all these have been prescribed to ensure that the king possesses the qualities by virtue of which he enjoys the universal respect and admiration and therefore also the strong allegiance of the people of his realm.[20]

DUTIES OF THE KING IN THE SMRTIS

The smrti-writers present a list of kingly duties. Protection of the subjects is considered to be his primary duty, and it is suggested that he should provide equal protection to all. In this connection Manu states that the king is bound to protect his subjects, as he will be rewarded created king for the sake of providing protection.[21] The other smrti-writers and sutra-writers too consider protective duty as the primary and the compulsory duty of the king.[22]

This protective duty signifies several types of functions. Visnu prescribes the protection of the seven constituent

17. Manu, VII, 45, 47-49.
18. Yaj. I.1 309-11.
19. Kat. 1-2.
20. Visnu, III. 50-51.
21. Manu, VII. 144: VIII. 3.
22. Gaut, Dh. S. X. 47; Vasdh, S. XIX. 1L Bound, Dh. S. 1.10.18.1: Visnu, V. 70: Nar. XVIII, 33: also SP. LVII, III.

elements of the state.[23] One of the important duties of the king is to eliminate the danger of the destruction of the kingdom. The sovereignty and integrity of the kingdom is to be protected because upon that depends the prosperity of the people, and a kingdom can prosper only when it is well protected. In the early centuries of the Christian era wars and invasions were frequent. Therefore, our smrti-writers took every precaution to protect the elements of the state. Manu states that if the kingdom be securely protected by the strength of the king's arms, it will constantly flourish like a well watered tree.[24]

Not only external aggression is a threat to the integrity of the kingdom but internal disturbances may also prove fatal. Being conscious of this fact our smrti -writers ask the king to maintain internal peace which contributes to the prosperity of the state. The law-givers apprehended different kinds of threat to internal peace. Visnu says that if anybody throws into another man's should pay a fine of pana.[25]

The smrtis refer to some undesirable persons whose presence causes harm to society and advice the king to eliminate them. Manu divides such persons onto two categories, open cheats and concealed rogues. The first subsists by cheating in the sale of various marketable commodities, but the second acts as burglars, robbers in forests and so forth. Manu presents another list of persons who cause harm to people by their undesirable conduct. He speaks of those who take bribes, cheat, act as rogues, gamble and live by performing auspicious ceremonies. He also refers to sanctimonious hypocrites and fortune-tellers, officials of higher ranks and physicians who act improperly, men who live by showing their proficiency in arts and clever harlots.[26]

Yajnavalkya presents another list of such persons and suggests that the king should provide protection to the subjects against them. They are cheats, thieves and men of

---

23. Visnu, III. 33.
24. Manu, IX, 255.
25. Visnu, V. 110.
26. Manu, IX, 257, 259.

bad livelihood and violent deeds. He also adds that subjects should be specially protected from kayasthas or revenue officials.[27]

That the king was also the protector of human dignity becomes quite evident from Visnu's rule to the effects that those persons who humiliate others have to pay fine, its amount varying according to the nature of case.[28]

Protection of the property of subjects was another important duty of the king. It is apparent that the institution of property was well established during the early centuries of the Christian era and that people possessed movable as well as immovable property. Sometimes citizens kept their property in the form of deposit for the sake of safety. These deposits could be either attested or unattested and in the latter case a wicked man might refuse to return the property. In such a situation the king is asked to punish the culprit.[29] It is laid down that immovable property shall also be protected by the king. Manu prescribes that if anybody demolishes a house or a peace of ground he shall have to pay a fine of the second amercement.[30] the king is made particularly responsible for protection of the property of certain special categories of persons. Heirless property shall be protected by the king for three years. If the owner claims his property during this period, it is to be returned to him. But if the property remains unclaimed for this period the king may possess.[31]

Minor's property is to be protected by the king as they are unfit for legal transactions.[32]

Besides the king was also the protector of the property belonging to certain classes of women. Manu says that those women who are barren, those who have no sons, those who are wives and widows faithful to their lords and women afflicted with diseases, have the right to get their properties

27. Yaj. 1, 336.
28. Visnu, V. 60-68.
29. Nar. I.7.
30. Manu, V.108.
31. *Ibid.*, VIII. 30; Ap, Dh. S. 11.6.14.5.
32. Manu, VIII, 27; Vas, Dh, S. XVI.8.

protected by the king.[33] Vasistha holds that only widow's property should be protected by the king.[34] But on the whole the king is assigned a special

Responsibility for protecting the property of those women who cannot be supported by the husbands, sons and others for some reason or the other.

The economic system of the country then retained certain types of common property also, and it was king's task to protect that property. Visnu stresses the importance of pastoral property and states that animals, domestic and wild, are to be protected. According to this law-giver pastoral property included elephants, horses, camels, cows and the killer of these had to lose one hand or one foot.[35] Manu also vices the same idea when he states that animals and pastoral ground should be protected.[36]

Vegetation constituted wealth, and hence much care was taken to protect it. Such a view is expressed particularly by Visnu, which says that the king is responsible for protecting trees which yield fruit and the feller of such trees deserves the highest amercement as fine. The feller of trees yielding blossoms has to pay a fine amounting to the second amercement. The cutter of creepers, shrubs and plants had to pay a hundred karsapanas. Even the cutter of grass is to be fined one karsapana.[37]

Royal responsibility was extended to the protection of agricultural produce. Visnu states that if anybody steals the crops, which grow in the rainy season, he shall pay eleven times its value as fine. He who steals the winter crops such as rice and barley shall pay eleven times its value as fine.[38] Thus the king was required to keep an eye on the harvest of the two crops corresponding to the rabi and kharif of later times.

---

33. *Ibid.*
34. Vas, Dh. S. XVI. 8.
35. Visnu, V. 111; V. 48-54: V. 255-59.
36. Manu, VIII, 230-37.
37. Visnu, V. 55-59.
38. *Ibid.*, V. 79-80

The caste system was a unique feature of the brahmanical society. It was thought that non-fulfilment of the functions assigned to different castes would result in disaster. Therefore the king was entrusted with the duty of upholding the social order based on the caste system.

Manu states that the main task of the king is to prevent the confusion of castes.[39] Narada and others also advise the king to compel the different castes to discharge the duties assigned to them.[40] The Santi Parva as well as certain Dharmasutras indicate that the king is the protector of the social order.[41] Such an instruction can be appreciated of one considers the context of foreign invasions which caused danger to the whole brahmanical social order.

During the early centuries of the Christian era trade and commerce flourished, but all this happened under the guidance of the authority of the state. The king regulated trade and commerce in different ways. First, the sale of the different commodities in the market was regulated by the king. Visnu and Yajnavalkya demand that the sale of forbidden food and liquor should be prohibited by the king and punishment of high amercement be inflicted for any violation.[42] The sale of adulterated food was considered a crime, and was to be punished.

The defects of an article or selling old articles after having repaired them, he shall compel the merchant to give their double quantity to the purchaser and would charge a fine equal to the value of the article.[43]

Yajnavalkya says that a person who adulterates drug, or oily commodities or salt, or perfumes, or paddy or sugar or other salable articles, shall be fined sixteen panas. He condemns all cheating in selling any kind of product. He lays sown that for making one sort of article appear as another

39. Manu, VIII. 122, 33.
40. Nar. XVIII. 33: Visnu, III. 3: AS. BK. III. CH. 1
41. SP. X. 36: Vas. Dh.S, XIX, 78 : Ap. Dh. S.11. 10. 27. 18: Gaunt, DH. S. XI. 9.
42. Visnu, V. 49, 173-74: Yaj. II. 245.
43. Manu, IX. 386: Br. XXII. 7.

sort, whether it be earthen goods, or skins, or precious stones, or trees or corn or wood or bark of trees, or clothes, the merchant shall have to pay a fine amounting to eight times the price. The king was expected to regulate all prices and prohibit arbitrary and unreasonable price.

The King should fix the price in such a manner that it might help both the purchaser and the seller, making allowance for the cost of the article together with other charges relating to the commodity.[44] Merchants were allowed neither to sell the commodities at a price lower than the prescribed one nor at a higher price. This is the opinion of Visnu[45] and it indicates that the state fixed process for various categories of commodities.

The amount of profit was also fixed by the state. Yajnavalkya states that the price in sale and purchase is regulated by the king and the difference is declared to be the dealer's profit.[46] It is obvious that all the provisions mentioned above were meant to put a check upon merchants and traders who were prone to cheating the consumers in every way.

Acquisistion of wealth was another duty of the king. Manu and Yajnavalkya say that his primary economic duty is the acquisition of wealth. Both instruct the king to protect what he has acquired, increase it and then deposit it with deserving persons.[47]

The inspection of income and expenditure by king was also advised. Yajnavalkya included this in the daily routine of the king, which emphasizes the importance of the duty.[48] Collection of revenue was another financial duty of the king.[49]

Our smrti-writers are conscious of the fact that certain unsocial elements might disturb the internal peace. Their elimination was desirable so that the moral standards could

---

44. Yaj. II. 245, 246, 253.
45. Visnu, V. 125-26.
46. Yaj. II. 251.
47. Manu, VII. 112: Yaj. I. 317, 327.
48. *Ibid.*, I. 327.
49. Manu, VII. 80.

be maintained. Yajnavalkya states that the king should punish the takers of bribes after having deprived them of their wealth.[50] Brhaspati prescribes banishment for those who are malicious, cause dissension or indulge in violent acts or who are inimicably disposed towards the king.[51] And their friends were considered to be unsocial elements and it was essential to banish them. The king should detect with the help of his spies the persons who steal the belongings of the people directly or indirectly. In order to catch the thieves the king's attendants may either associate themselves with thieves or spot them by marks of their criminality or by the possession of their stolen goods.[52]

Our smrti-writers assign certain political functions to the king like making several appointments including the religious ones. Several law-givers agree that the king should appoint officiating priests who would help him in offering sacrifices.[53] Besides the purohita, ministers were also appointed by the king, although the earliest law-givers do not speak of this royal function. Judges and a band of civil servants were appointed by the king to render assistance to him in the discharge of his multifarious duties.

The king was responsible for the preservation of the culture and tradition of society. His duty extends to the protection of public or religious places so that they are not demolished or put in an unsanitary condition. Manu warns that he who destroys a bridge, a pole, or images, shall repair the whole damage and pay a fine of hundred panas.[54] Other places which should be protected by the king are assembly houses, places where water is distributed or cakes are sold, brothels, taverns, shops, crossroads assemblies, play houses, concert-rooms, old gardens, forests the shops of artisans, empty dwellings, natural and artificial groves, etc. as well as

50. Yaj. I. 33.
51. Br. XVII. 16.
52. Manu, IX. 256; Br. XXII. 3, XXI. 6 : Kat. 15.
53. Manu, VII 78: Yaj. I. 314: Kat. 24: Vas Dh. S. XIX, 2: Bau Dh. S. 1.10.18.7: Gant. Dh. S. XI. 12.
54. Manu, 1, IX. 285.

store houses, armories, temples, etc.[55] Yajnavalkya suggests that the king should grow trees at the places of memorial erections and disposal of the dead, on boundary lines, at places, or in temples.[56]

Pollution of public places was a crime. Except in some extreme cases, those dropping filth on the king's high road were required to pay a fine of two karsapanas and to immediately remove the filth.[57] But Visnu does not allow the pollution of public places under any circumstances. He states that if one defiles the highway, or a garden or the reservoirs of water by vomiting excrements near them or in any other way he shall be fined a hundred panas.[58] Brhaspati says that a passage by which men and animals go to and fro unhindered is called samsarnana and must not be obstructed by anyone nor polluted by spitting or in any other way.[59] This particular duty is not mentioned in the earliest law-books, and it might be an indication of the fact that with the passage of time the responsibilities of the king increased. According to him whoever throws dirt in the street shall be punished with a cine of one-eighth of a pana: whoever causes mire or water to collect in the street shall be fined one-fourth of a pana; whoever commits the above offences on the king's road shall be punished with double the fine. Further, he says that whoever excretes faces in places of pilgrimage, reservoirs of water, temples and royal buildings shall be punished with fines rising from one pana and upwards in the order to the offences, but when such excretions are due to the use of medicine or disease, no punishment shall be inflicted.[60]

In every society some persons need the help of others on account of their physical, mental or social disabilities. Our law-givers provide for such needy persons. Manu says that the king must treat kindly an srotriya, a sick person, a

---

55. *Ibid.*, IX. 280, 283.
56. Yaj. II. 238.
57. Manu, IX. 282.
58. Visnu, V. 106.
59. Br. XIX. 27, 28.
60. As. Bk. II. Ch. XXXVI.

distressed man, an infant or an aged or an indigent man, a man of high birth and an honorable man.[61] Gautama, an earlier lawgiver, expresses more or less a similar view. He states that srotriya, who are brahmanas and people who are unable to work, even or they are brahmana, needy temporary students, etc. are to be protected by the king.[62] Both Gautama and Manu include persons of a particular class to be protected by the state. Nevertheless in Visnu we come across and idea regarding the duty of the king to fine those persons who injure of strike a man unable it move about, eat or speak.[63] Here no caste consideration is shown. Katyayana too emphasizes that the king is the protector of the helpless, the house of the homeless, the son of the sonless, and father of the fatherless.[64] The Santi Parva states that the king should always support and protect the helpless, the lordless, the aged and widows.[65]

Sometimes on account of natural calamities people suffer a lot. Manu states that the king should help the people in both normal and abnormal fines, and during the period of famine, or distress reduce the tax burden.[66]

As dead of the state the king was vested with some judicial duties. Customs and traditions carried much weight in society and the king could not go against them. Yajnavalkya advises the king to personally investigate judicial proceedings daily in the company of his assessors.[67] The royal judicial duty included the awarding punishments to criminals. Visnu also insists that the king should punish that according to justice.[68] Narada says that no harm in some if the king punishes those who deserve punishment, for fire is not polluted even though it always burns the creatures of the world. He further shays that proper discharge of the judicial

61. *Ibid.*
62. Gaut. Dh. S. X. 10-14.
63. Visnu, V. 69.
64. P.V. Kane, HDS, Vol. III, pp. 23-33.
65. SP, 86, 24.
66. Manu, X. 118.
67. Yaj. I. 360.
68. Visnu, III. 96.

functions by the king would bring fame to him on this world and an everlasting residence in heaven.[69]

Visnu says that king enjoys the power to pardon the offenders. But at the same time Visnu imposes a limit also. If anybody commits a crime twice the king should not grant him pardon.[70]

Several conclusions may be drawn from the above concepts about the role of the king during the period represented by the smrtis. Firs, our smrti- writers emphasized the role and functions of the king primarily by way of his duties rather than his rights or powers. Secondly, in spite of the fact that monarchy was the established form of government, the king shall always to keep in mind that he ruled over the country not for his own sake but for the benefit of the people.

PERSONAL SAFETY OF THE KING IN THE SMRTIS

As the king was the upholder of the caste system, the protector of the life and liberty of the citizens and helper of the helpless, protection of his person was important and our smrti-writers gave applied their mind to this subject also. They presumed that the king might fall a prey to different kings of dangers, against which he must take care.

Among the smrti-writers Manu is the one who suggests some measures for the personal safety of the king. Friends both within and outside the country might be dangerous for the king. So he should be careful while choosing his friends. Manu greatly commends a weak friend who is righteous and grateful, whose people are contented and who is loyal and persevering in his undertakings. He suggests such friends because they would not be able to bluff the king. Manu also advises the king to keep his personal interest above everything. He states that let the king unhesitatingly quit for his own safety a county, although it be salubrious. Fertile and rich in cattle. He adds that in times of need let the king

69. Nar. XVIII. 17-18; 133.

70. Visnu, III. 93.

preserve his own wealth: at the expense of his wealth, let him preserve his wife; at all events he should preserve himself, even at the cost of his wife and wealth.[71]

Our smrti-writers were so particular regarding his personal security that they provide safety measures regarding the food meant for the king. Manu states that the king may eat food which has been prepared by the faithful and incorruptible (servants), who know the proper time for dining and which has been well examined and hallowed by the sacred tools that destroy poison. He also suggests that all the food meant for the king should be mixed with medicines that are antidotes of poison. He further advises precaution in the use of the dress and jewellery to be worn by the king. The king should always wear those gems, which destroy poison. Manu asks the king to be careful of those female servants who attends him at the time of his toilet. Well tried women, whose ornaments have been carefully examined, are to serve the king with fans, water and perfumes. Finally the king is required to be careful about his carriages, bed, seats, bath, toilet and all his ornaments.[72]

The meticulously detailed measures regarding the safety of the king laid down by the smrti-writers suggests that during the early centuries of the Christian era rivalries and violence of the usurpation of the throne was frequently apprehended and therefore the king had to be cautious in safeguarding his position and life.

THE POSITION OF THE KING IN SMRTIS

The various duties entrusted to the king prove his important place in society. In the absence of the king anarchy would prevail. Mentioning the disastrous consequences arising from the absence of the king Manu says: "when these creatures, being without a king, through fear dispersed in all directions, the lord created a king for the protection of this whole creation." Therefore in the opinion of smrti-writers the

71. Manu, VII. 209, 212-13.
72. *Ibid.*, VII. 217-20

presence of the king was indispensable for the well-being of the people. Hence the king is assigned the highest place in society. Manu states that the king is more powerful than fire which consumes only that man who approaches it, but the king destroys the whole family and all the belongings of the man who tries to harm him in any way. Manu does not empower the people to go against the king due to his divine nature. The king is so powerful that as soon as he gets any indication regarding this he destroys the enemy. Though Manu accepts that the king is a mortal, he supports his supreme authority over his subjects by setting that since he is a great deity in human form, even an infant king must not be shown disrespect.[73]

Narada too establishes the supremacy of the king in the garb of his divinity. He says that law personified a king roams on earth invisibly, with a thousand eyes. Mortals cannot live at all if they transgress his commandments. The king should command respect in every case whether he is efficient or not. Narada suggests that just as even a feeble husband must be respected by his subjects. Narada kept the brahmana and the king above the law of the land. He opines that a brahmana and a king could neither be questioned in a court of law nor could be given corporal punishment. Not only in the legal field but also in the economic field Narada establishes the supreme authority of the king. He states that as the king practices austerities he is supreme over subjects. His orders must be obeyed. People depend upon the king to earn their livelihood. According to Narada the king is the master of all the wealth in society. Through a simile he tries to strengthen his argument. He states that as pure and impure water becomes alike on their junction in the ocean, so all property impure and pure acquired by a king becomes pure in his hand. Narada declares that as gold, on being thrown into the blazing fire acquires purity, even so all gains become pure in the hands of kings.[74]

---

73. *Ibid.,* VII. 3, 8-9, 12.
74. Nar. XVIII. 20, 22, 25, 45-46.

The Dharmasutras also testify that the king occupies a very important place in society. Gautama states that all, except brahmanas, shall worship him who is seated on a high place while they themselves sit on a lower one.[75] He asks even the brahmanas to honour the king. However, Apastamba suggests a different idea regarding the position of the king: "The king should not occupy a superior position. He should not live better than his gurus or ministers."[76] This indicates that in the period represented by the Dharmasutra the king was not as powerful as he became in later times.

Several references indicate that our smrti-writers advocated royal absolution. It is held that Manu produced his law-book to support the absolute rule of Pusyamitra, a Sunga king. There are other references that indicate that the position of the king was not absolute. Our smrti-writers imposed various restrictions over the behaviour of the king. They never favoured the idea that the king should be a oppressor, and in their opinion an oppressive king would face bad consequences. Manu cautions that the king who oppresses would perish with his relatives and kingdom. He also says that the lives of living creatures are destroyed by oppressing their kingdom.[77]

In the financial field to restrictions were imposed. The king was advised not to impose unjust taxes. The treasury should not be filled by unjust methods. Katyayana states that the king who unjustly collects from his kingdom taxes, fines, share of crops and tolls incurssin.[78] Yajnavalkya warns that the sovereign who enriches his treasury by illegal exactions is soon bereft of good luck and goes to destruction along with his kinsmen. Yajnavalkya also adds that the fire arising form the heart of the subjects does not cease without destroying the family, fortune and life of the King.[79] Visnu puts another restriction over the king which we do not find in other smrtis: "And let him not injure his own property (by bootless

75. Gaunt, Dh.S, XI. 7.
76. Ap. Dh. S. 11.10.25.10.
77. Manu, VII. 111-12.
78. Kat. 19.
79. Yaj. I. 340-41.

expenses)."[80] It means that the king should not to be whimsical in spending his own property.

In the judicial field also the activities of the king were restricted. It is true that in a way the king was supreme in the judicial field. His authority was final in so far as inflicting of punish of punishment as concerned. But here also he had to be guided by moral principle.

The king is advised to decide the cases of people according to the rules of the Sastras, but at the same time Katyayana also enjoins that in the absence of sacred texts he should carry out he judicial administration according to the usages of the country. It means that the king could not decide cases arbitrarily. Besides this the king should also inflict punishment properly.[81] Manu also advises the king not to award punishment in an arbitrary manner. He states that having fully considered the time and the place of the offence, the strength and the knowledge of the offender, the king should inflict just punishment on the man who acts unjustly.[82]

The king's conduct was regulated not in his own country but also in the defeated countries. Our smṛti-writers did not allow the king to rule over those countries in an arbitrary manner. Yajnavalkya advises him that whatever be the custom, laws and family usage in a country they should be observed by him when the country has come under his control.[83]

In conclusion we can say that all these limitations were moral limitation, the violation of which did not lead to any legal action against the king. It is not clear how far these limitations were accepted by the king. It is probable that our smrti-writers painted the picture of an ideal king.

80. Visnu, III.52.
81. Kat. 45. 960.
82. Manu, VII.16.
83. Yaj. I.343.

Chapter

3

Mantri Parishad

Monarchy was the accepted form of government during the period of the smrtis. This however does not mean that the king carried on the duties of the state single-handed. Perhaps our smrtikars were aware that absolute power corrupts absolutely. It was also realized that for administrative convenience the rule by one person is never preferable. Emphasizing the importance of ministers Kautilya points out: "Kingship is possible only with the aid of assistants, a single wheel cannot work (a chariot) ; therefore the king should APPOINT MINISTERS AND LISTEN TO THEIR OPINION."[1] Manu also states that tit is difficult for a person to accomplish single handed even an easy task; how can government, particularly one which has great good as its aim, be run without helpers?[2] It appears that as administration became complex due to the increased responsibilities of the king it was advisable for him to consult other persons while discharging them.

There is no agreement over the number of ministers among the law-givers. Kautilya quotes the opinion of some

1. AS, BK. I. Ch. VII.
2. Manu, VII. 55.

other authorities on this point. First, he quotes Manu who opines that the king should appoint twelve ministers. Brhaspati preferred a council of sixteen ministers, and Usanas says that twenty ministers should be included in the Mantri Parishad. But Kautilya seems to be more practical and he does not specify the number of ministers to be appointed by the king. He only rules that the number of ministers should be as many as the needs of the dominion required.[3] Manu prescribes only of eight ministers.[4] Perhaps he thought that a big council would become an unwieldy body in which proper deliberations would not be possible. Yajnavalkya, however, is silent on the question of the number of ministers to be appointed by the king.[5] R.C. Majumdar thinks that though the number of ministers was not definitely fixed. Manu's recommendation of seven or eight ministers may have been followed at times. He doubts whether such a central mantri parishad comparable to parishad of the Maurya inscriptions existed. He also says that if such an institution did exist it does not find prominent mention in the epigraphs. To H.C. Raychaudhuri it seems that the sabhas referred to in the Allahabad pillar inscription in connection with the nomination scene of Samudra Gupta may have been courtiers attending a durbar as well as members of a central council.[6]

APPOINTMENT OF THE MINISTERS

The king was the sole appointing authority according to all smrti-writers. But he could not exercise unlimited authority for smrti-writers were cautious enough to prescribe the qualities, which a minister must possess.

First, almost all smrti-writers agreed that ministers must be native, born of high family, influential, well trained in arts, possessed of foresight, wise, of string memory, bold eloquent, skilful, intelligent, possessed of enthusiasm, dignity and endurance, pure in character, affable, firm, loyal,

3. AS, BK. I, Ch. X.
4. Manu, VII. 54.
5. Yaj. I. 312.
6. An Advanced History of India, I, p. 193.

devoted, endowed with excellent conduct, strength, death and bravery, free from procrastination, fickle-mindedness, affectionate, and free from such qualities as excite, hatred and enmity.[7] Yajnavalkya opines that ministers should be intelligent, steady and pure.[8] Visnu suggests that ministers should be pure, free from covetousness, attractive and able.[9]

It seems that all these qualities are enumerated in order to inspire the people to respect the ministers. Yajnavalkya prescribes that ministers should be hereditary servants.[10] Perhaps Manu also favours this idea. He states that their ancestors should have been royal servants.[11] Epigraphic sources prove that hereditary qualification was taken into consideration at the time of the appointment of ministers.

Specialists in the different fields were appointed as ministers. Manu advises the king to appoint those persons as ministers who are versed in the sciences and who are heroes as well as skilled in the use of weapons.[12]

Consideration of Varna weighed heavily with the law-givers. The lower castes were excluded from civil service. R.S. Sharma holds that the organization of bureaucracy, which was an important instrument of the state apparatus and which was covered by the term amatya in the saptanga theory of the state, seems to have been based on caste.[13] Some epigraphic evidences prove that certain posts were occupied by Vaisyas or Sudras also. The Karitlai Plates of Maharaja Jayanatha[14] (a Gupta inscription of AD 493-4) refers to initiate householder named Sarvadatta who was an uparika (provincial governor) and a dutaka (executor of grants), R.S. Sharma opines that since this officer is described as the

7. AS, BK. I, Ch. IX.
8. Yaj. I. 312.
9. Visnu, III. 71.
10. Yaj. I. 312.
11. Manu, VII. 54.
12. *Ibid.*, VII. 54.
13. R.S. Sharma, Aspects of Political Ideas and Institutions in Ancient India, p. 164.
14. CII, III. No. 26, p. 120.

master of masons (sthapati-samrat) perhaps he was a Vaisya or a Sudra.[15]

Katyayana favours the idea that brahmana should be appointed as a minister.[16] Yajnavalkya does not say anything specific about it, but he says that the king must consult the brahmana.[17]

It is likely that brahmanas enjoyed dominance in the Mantri Parishad. From a verse of Manu we can construe that he was in favour of giving representation to the different castes of the society. He holds that such as are versed in the sciences, and heroes skilled in the use of weapons, etc. should be appointed ministers.[18] Nobility of birth also is urged as consideration by Kautilya and Manu.[19]

Katyayana lays down devotion towards the king as a qualification for holding the post of a minister.[20]

FEATURES OF THE MANTRI PARISHAD

We have some idea about the way in which the Mantri Parishad was expected to function. Secrecy concerning its proceedings was the most important feature and the law-givers suggest several measures to safeguard it. To emphasize the importance of secrecy, Kautilya advises even the exclusion of parrots, dogs and other animals because they divulge secrets.[21] The presence of unauthorized persons at the time of consultation is not allowed by Kautilya.[22] Manu suggests that the meeting should be held in a secluded place.[23] He further vices the same opinion when he says that the meeting must be held at the back of a hill or terrace, in a lonely place or

15. R.S. Sharma, Aspects of Political Ideas and Institutions in Ancient India, p. 167.
16. Kat. II.
17. Yaj. I, 312.
18. Manu, VII. 54.
19. AS, BK. I, Ch. IX: Manu, VII. 34.
20. Kat. II.
21. AS, BK. I, Ch. XV.
22. *Ibid.*, BK. I, Ch. XV.
23. Manu, VII. 147.

in a solitary forest.[24] Manu also prohibits the presence of some persons in the meeting as they were liable to disclose the secrets. He rules that idiots, the dumb, the blind and the deaf, animals, very aged men, women, barbarians, the sick and those deficient in limbs, should not be allowed to be present in the meeting as they were liable to disclose the secrets.[25]

Furthermore he also forbids the presence of animals and at the same time enjoins that as 'particularly women betray secret counsel' and ' for that reason he must be careful with respect to them.'[26]

What was the importance of the secret counsel? In the opinion of Kautilya the divulgence of secret counsel is fatal to the security and well-being of the king and the officers appointed by him.[27] Manu justifies the secrecy of the cabinet proceedings on the found that it enables that king to enjoy the pleasures of the world, even though he may be poor in treasure.[28] Yajnavalkya admits the importance of secret deliberations when he states that because a kingdom has its roots in mantra it should be well guarded and may not get any inkling of it till its results been achieved.[29]

Different categories of ministers act in the council. Chief ministers as well as the other ministers took part in its deliberations.

The king consulted the ministers while discharge his several duties. Manu suggests that the king should confer with the ministers individually so that they should express their opinion freely. After that he should try to consult them together to know the opinion of the whole cabinet. Kautilya favoured the idea of the two types of deliberations.[30] Manu favours individual as well as joint deliberations.[31]

---

24. *Ibid.*, VI. 149.
25. *Ibid.*, VII. 149.
26. *Ibid.*, VII. 150.
27. AS, BK. I, Ch. XV.
28. Manu, VII. 148.
29. Yaj. I, 344.
30. AS, BK, I, Ch. XV.
31. Manu, VII. 57.

There is no clear-cut description of the meetings of the Mantri Parishad in the smrtis. Kautlya refers to the two types of meetings, ordinary as well as emergency. In the emergency meeting ordinary councilors and members of the Mantri Parishad were called.[32] Certain verses of Manu too indicate that both ordinary and emergency meetings were held. He states that in daily meetings ordinary business was discussed.[33] Another verse of Manu suggests that certain emergency meetings were also held. He advises that with the most distinguished among the ministers, i.e. brahmana, let the king deliberate on the most important affairs which relate to the six measures of royal policy.[34]

The meetings were presided over by the king though Manu provides that in the absence of the king the chair may be taken by the chief minister.[35]

JURISDICTION OF THE MANTRI PARISHAD

Manu presents a list of topics which should be discussed by the Mantri Parishad. He advise the king to consider daily with them the ordinary business referring to peace and war, the four subjects called sthana, the revenue, the manner of protecting himself and his kingdom, and sanctification of his gains by pious gift.[36] Furthermore he enjoins that the matters concerning marriage of daughters and protection of his sons from harm,[37] the dispatch of ambassadors, completion of the undertakings already begun and conduction women in his harem, are some of the matters over which the king should have consultations.[38] Besides this the king should also consult his ministers over matters concerning foreign affairs such as the doings of his spies.[39]

---

32. AS, BK. I. Ch. XV.
33. Manu, VII. 56.
34. *Ibid.*, VII. 58.
35. *Ibid.*, VII. 141.
36. *Ibid.*, VII. 56.
37. *Ibid.*, VII. 152.
38. *Ibid.*, VII. 153.
39. *Ibid.*, VII 153.

the whole eight-fold businesses, the five classes of spies, the goodwill or enmity and the conduct of the neighbours,[40] the conduct of middle most prince, the doings of persons who seek conquest, the behaviour of the neutral king and on that of the foe, etc.[41]

These verses indicate that the Mantri Parishad discussed a wide range of subjects which included personal as well as public matters. It seems that these ministers were managing the affairs concerning the relationship with other states. It also seems that a particular minister was in-charge of spies.

Besides this a particular minister was in-charge of the local affairs. Manu entrusts a minister with the duty of inspecting the business of the local bodies. That minister must be loyal.[42] The Mahabharata also confirms that some pious ministers should carefully supervise the administrative officers and the mutual relations of those officers.[43]

That these ministers were entrusted with the judicial duties becomes evident from certain texts. Manu suggests that when the king is tried with the inspection of men let him place of that seat his chief minister who must be acquainted with the law, wise, self-controlled and descended from a noble family.[44] A verse of Katyayana informs us that ministers along with the king participated in the judicial proceedings. Katyayana adds that the king who looks into causes according to the sacred law along with the judge, the ministers, the brahmanas, the family priest and the assessors obtain heaven.[45] Another verse of Katyayana also to hell by not punishing sinners and punishing those who bow to the law.[46]

Sometimes ministers assisted the king when he was in his recreations. Yajnavalkya describing the daily routine of

---

40. *Ibid.*, VII. 154.
41. *Ibid.*, VII. 155.
42. *Ibid.*, VII. 120.
43. SP, 87.10.
44. Manu, VII. 141.
45. Kat. 56.
46. *Ibid.*, 961.

the king, advise him to divert himself alone or in the company of his ministers. The Mataksara explains that in the afternoon "as he may like" following his own fancy, alone "let him divert" himself "in his interior apartments." It further says that the king should enjoy in the company of his ministers, who are confidential, skilled in arts such as (music) and who are buffoons and jesters.[47] The epigraphic sources show that ministers were concerned with the construction and excavation work also. The Udayagiri cave inscription of Chandra Gupta II describes the excavation of the cave as a temple of God Siva, under the name of Sambhu, by the order of a certain Vurasena otherwise called Saba who was one of the ministers of Chandra Gupta II.[48] The Junagadh rock-inscription of Skanda Gupta speaks of the construction of the embankment on the lake Sudersana. It states that the lake Sudersana had burst in consequence o excessive rain and so the embankment was constructed by the orders of Cakrapalita after two month's work, in the Gupta year one hundred and thirty seven, i.e. 456-57 AD.[49]

RELATIONSHIP BETWEEN THE KING AND THE MANTRI PARISHAD

The subjects over which the king carried on consolation with his ministers sometimes create an impression that the Mantri Parishad occupied a pivotal position in the administrative set-up of the country. But in actuality it occupied a secondary place. The king was all-powerful. Although the king consulted the Mantri Parishad on each and every matter, he was not bound to accept the advice tendered by them. It depended upon the king to accept or to reject the advice. Manu prescribes that the king should always entrust to his official all business; having taken his final resolution with him let him afterwards begin to act.[50] So the final

47. Yaj. I. 329.
48. CII, III, No. 6, pp. 34-35.
49. *Ibid.*, III. No. 14, pp. 63-64.
50. Manu, VII. 59.

authority was of the king and not that of the ministers. Manu further rules: "whatever matter his ministers or the judge may settle improperly, the king himself shall resettle and fine the erring ministers one thousand panas."[51] From this verse we can derive two conclusions. First, though the ministers were entitled to settle matters concerning their departments, their decision was not the final. Appeal against their decision could be made to the king, whose decision was considered to be final; Secondly, ministers could be fined also for not carrying on their duties properly. Yajnavalkya too does not vest final authority to the ministers. He suggests that in consolation with them, he should administer the kingdom so also with the brahmanas, and thereafter himself. The Mitaksara explains that having thus previously appointed his ministers the king should administer, in consultation with them all. Or with some of them, the matters relating to his kingdom, such as making treaties, declaring war, etc. In this way after knowing their opinion, and after consulting with a brahmana, who is expert in the knowledge of all Sastras and their meaning viz. after consulting his purohita, let him "act himself" according to his own reason and understanding.[52] In conclusion it can be said that king's ministers were not his colleagues but they were merely his subordinates.

51. *Ibid.*, IX. 234.
52. Yaj. I. 312.

Chapter

4

Lok Sewaks

Our smrti-writer quote conscious of the fact that administration of a state could not be run by the king efficiently until and unless he was assisted by a band of Lok Sewaks other than the ministers. In our texts we do not get any clear indication of the importance of the Lok Sewaks but the smrti portion of the Mahabharata, states that there is no wealth more valuable to kings than the proper selection of servants.[1] It can not be denied that upon the efficiency of the Lok Sewaks depends the healthy functioning of the whole administrative system. Being conscious of these realities the smrti-writers provide that able Lok Sewaks should be employed by the king to assist him in discharging his multifarious duties.

The king was the sole appointing authority and he appointed Lok Sewaks from top to bottom. It seems that he enjoyed the power of dismissal also. The smrti-writers do not fix the number of Lok Sewaks, as they do in the case of ministers. Manu advises the king to appoint as many persons as the due performance of his business requires.[2]

1. SP. 56.34.
2. Manu, VII.61.

CATEGORIES OF LOK SEWAKS, THEIR QUALIFICATIONS AND DUTIES

As the duties of the king during the early centuries of the Christian era had increased he required the help of a large number of Lok Sewaks. Therefore, we find the description of the different categories of Lok Sewaks who were assigned various functions.

Smrti-writers prescribe certain general and specific qualifications for Lok Sewaks. Stating the general qualifications Manu says that officers should possess integrity, wisdom, firmness and ability to collect money, they should be well tried.[3] The Santi Parva provides a comprehensive list of the personal qualities of Lok Sewaks viz., they should be brave, devoted and not amenable to the influence of enemies, healthy, well behaved, never unmindful of future life, always observant of their duties, honest and form like mountains.[4] In addition to these, special qualifications are laid down for various types of functionaries. First, for instance a purohita had to be appointed to assist the king in discharging his sacrificial duty. Offering sacrifice was essential for the king to ensure his prosperity in this world as well as in the other world after his death. But the procedure of the sacrifice was so complex that the king was unable to perform that work single-handed. Manu advises the king to appoint a domestic priest (purohita) and to choose an officiating priest (rtvig). They shall perform the king's domestic rites and the sacrifices for which three fires are required.[5] It seems that the two categories of priests, purohita and rtvig did not have anything to do with the secular functions of the king. Manu does not specify any qualification which a purohita should possess. But Yajnavalkya and Katyayana enumerate certain qualities of the purohita. Yajnavalkya states the king should appoint a purohita, who is an astrologer, who is highly exalted, who is

3. *Ibid.*, VII. 60.
4. SP, 57 23-25.
5. Manu, VII. 78.

well versed in the theory of punishment as well as versed in the knowledge of the Atharvaveda.[6] All this does not necessarily mean that a purohita has to be a brahmana. But Katyayana advises the king to appoint a brahmana as his purohita, "who is highly spoken of (by the learned), who is well disposed, endowed with perfect Vedic learning, who is not greedy and who speaks the truth."[7] Likewise, Visnu too suggests certain qualifications. He instructs the king to appoint a man conversant with the Vedas, epics, the statutes of sacred law and the science of what is useful in life, is of a good family, not deficient in limbs and persistent in the practice of austerities.[8] It should be noted that both Katyayana and Visnu recommend the presence of certain physical traits besides learning and noble lineage. These bodily requirements are not laid down by Yajnavalkya. His suggestion that the purohita should be well versed on the theory of punishments means that by the fourth century AD domestic priest had started sharing the judicial responsibility of the king.

The Dharmasastras advise the king to appoint a purohita and they also enumerate his qualifications and duties. They opine that when kings are assisted by the brahmanas, they do not face difficulties. Gautama prescribes: "And he shall select as is domestic priest (purohita) a brahmana who is learned (in the Vedas), of noble family, eloquent, handsome, of (a suitable) age, and of a virtuous disposition, who lives righteously and who is austere. With his assistance he shall fulfil his religious duties. For it is declared (in the Vedas): 'Ksatriyas who are assisted by the Brahmanas, prosper and do not fall into distress."[9] Apastamba, who discussing the duties of a householder, asks the king to send such persons as transgress their order to his domestic priest, who should be learned in the law and the science of governing.[10] Apastamba shows that the purohita

6. Yaj. I. 313.
7. Kat. 24.
8. Visnu, III. 70.
9. Ganuty, Dh. S. XI. 12-14.
10. Ap. Dh. S. II. 5.11.14.

was associated with the work of penance. He rules: "A spiritual teacher, an officiating priest, a snataka, and a prince shall be able to protect a criminal from punishment by their inter-cession, except in case of a capital offence."[11] Baudhayana suggests that the king should choose a domestic priest who shall be foremost in all transactions.[12] Further he instructs the king to act according to the instructions of the purohita.[13] According to Vasistha the king should appoint a domestic priest to perform the rites obligatory for householders.[14] Emphasizing the importance of purohita in the administrative set-up he states that it is declared in the Veda, "A realm where a brahmana is appointed domestic priest, prospers."[15]

To sum up all these points it can be said that the domestic priest occupied an important place in the administrative set-up of the king. It is true that judged from the modern concepts of civil service in secular set-up a putohita can not strictly be considered it be a civil servant. But the period under study is one in which theological concepts are blended with secular ones and it is the total impact of these intertwined concepts which dominate even the state affairs in daily life. Thus in a religious society where secularism had hardly emerged, and where punishment and penance were both effective means to mitigate crime, the role of purohita must be treated as that of a civil servant of the then state.

Apart from the purohita several other functionaries assisted the king in his secular duties. The king was responsible for looking after the financial matters of the state, but he appointed certain other officers who helped him in the financial transactions. Though levying of taxes was the prerogative of the king, his officers collected the revenue. Manu rules: "Let him cause the annual revenue in his kingdom to be collected by trusty (officials)."[16]

---

11. *Ibid.*, II. 10.27.11.
12. Bound. Dh. S. I. 10.18.7.
13. *Ibid.*, I. 10.18.8.
14. Vas. Dh.S, XIX. 3.
15. *Ibid.*, XIX 4.
16. Manu, VII. 80.

Yajnavalkya too asks the king to appoint supervisors who are skilful, pure and expert in matters of income and expenditure.[17] The Mitaksara explains the various terms like they should be 'expert' not devoted to any other occupation, 'skilful' or master of that particular occupation, 'pure', i.e. free from four sorts of vices. Further, it also states that matters of income means the knowledge of those places which are sources of income such as gold mines, etc. According to it the matters of expenditure means the proper ways in which gold should be used.[18]

Mines and the other sources of national wealth belonged to the king, and officers were appointed by him to look after them. Manu states that the brave, the skilful, the highborn, and the honest in offices for the collection of revenues, in mines, manufactures and sore houses should be appointed by the king.[19] Visnu too refers to such office.[20] It was the most important duty of the king to protect the citizens from the houses in village the king should make the thief catchers had to pay from their own pocket or from some other funds available to them for this purpose.[21] Manu specks of guardsmen and vessals whose main duty was to protect the provinces from the thieves. If they failed to do that the king could punish them like thieves.[22] For protecting certain special places, like old gardens, forests, public water houses, etc. the police force of both kinds, stationary and patrolling, has to be maintained, according to Manu.[23]

Judiciary formed an important branch of administration. Although the king himself dispensed justice, the assistance of some officers was required for the proper working of the judicial organization. Especially Katyayana, Narada and Brhaspati refer to some officers who seems to

17. Yaj. II. 322.
18. *Ibid.*, XIII. 322.
19. Manu, VII. 62.
20. Visnu, III. 16
21. Kat. 813-14.
22. Manu, IX. 271
23. *Ibid.*, IX. 264-66.

belong to the Judicial service of that period. Katyayana mentions two officers Stobhaka and Sucaka. The Stohbaka is declared to be one who, with the sole eye to money and without being urged by the king, first informs him of a matter which is censored by Sastra (sacred law).[24]

Explaining the position and functions of the Sucaka Katyayana says that this officer is appointed by the king himself for discovering the wrong doings of others and reporting them to the king.[25] In order to record the deposition of the plaintiff or the defendant Katyayana recommends the appointment of one scribe.[26]

Analyzing the constitution of the court Brhaspati states that the accountant should compute the sum in dispute; the scribe should record the proceedings, the king's own officer should compel the attendance of the defendant, assessors and witnesses.[27] In the following two verses Brhaspati enumerates certain personal qualities for these offices. He opines that a virtuous man, who pays obedience to the judges, should be appointed by the king as his own officer to summon and to keep in custody the witnesses, plaintiff and defendant.[28] In the same way two persons thoroughly familiar with grammar and vocabulary, skilled in the art of computation, honest and acquainted with the various modes of writing should be appointed by the king as accountant and scribe respectively.[29] Narada indicates certain features of the constitution of the court, consisting of the king, his dutiful officer, the assessors of the court, the law book, the accountant and scribe, gold, fire and water: therefore it is said to have eight members.[30]

We get references to some other officials in scattered versed. Visnu presents a list of such officials. He ask the king to appoint able officials for the working of his mines, for the

24. Kat. 33.
25. *Ibid.*, 34.
26. *Ibid.*, 132.
27. Br. I. 8.
28. *Ibid.*, I. 15.
29. *Ibid.*, I. 14.
30. Nar. I. 15.

levying of taxes and of the fares at the ferries and also advises the king appoint pious persons for performing acts of piety such as bestowing gifts on the indignant and the like, skilled and for financial business such as examining gold and other precious metals; brave me for fighting; and eunuchs of his wives.[31] The Dharmasutras speak of some Lok Sewaks to whom there is no reference in smrtis. Apastamba mentions a civil servant who looked after the assembly house. His duty was to make arrangement for the various games that were going to be played there.[32] Another officer was appointed for looking after the crops in the fields so that they could not be destroyed by cattle.[33] Protection of the forests was also one of the duties of the king.[34]

The king had to maintain good relations with the other nations, and this necessitated the appointment of ambassadors. The smrti writers advised the king to appoint such persons very cautiously. Manu states that the ambassadors must be well versed in all sciences. He must be so clever that he can understand the hints and expressions of the face and gestures. Apart from these he must be honest, skilful and should belong to a noble family.[35] Manu further says that the candidate for ambassadorship should be loyal, honest, skilful, handsome, fearless and honest, and should know the proper place and time for action.[36] The enumeration of such qualities amply prove that men of high caliber and impressive appearance should be appointed as ambassadors. In the Garuda Purana too we notice more or less similar ideas regarding the qualifications of an ambassador. It states that the royal ambassador shall be a man of profound intelligence and clear comprehension. An adept in the art of stimulation, he must be able to read what passes in other

31. Visnu, III. 16-21.
32. Ap. Dh. S. 11.10.25.12.
33. *Ibid.*, 11.11.28.5.
34. *Ibid.*, 11.11.29.6.
35. Manu, VII. 63.
36. *Ibid.*, VII. 64.

men's mind, and of giving the right reply at the opportune moment.[37] Manu also states that ambassadors should maintain peace and declare war.[38] They are supposed to win as well as alienate allies.[39]

For the administrative efficiency the king maintained secret service also. We find the reference to spies in Manu[40] and Yajnavalkya.[41] These spies were concerned with both internal and external matters. Though these spies the king could learn about the corruption prevailing among the Lok Sewaks and thus eradicate this.[42]

What has been stated above creates the impression that there was a network of Lok Sewaks who were appointed on the basis of personal qualifications. The king exercised tight control over them. They could not exploit the general people. It seems that our smrti-writers were quite conscious of the vices of bureaucracy. They apprehended that Lok Sewaks might take bribe from the citizens, which would corrupt the whole administrative system. Therefore, they insist that Lok Sewaks must be free form vices. Manu opines that officers should be free from sloth.[43] the description of the vices of Lok Sewaks is also found in Dharmasutras, and it is stressed that the king should not be surrounded by such officials. Vasistha says that a king will not be exalted if he lives surrounded by servants who are greedy like vultures.[44] The Garuda Purana mentions that a man bereft of all fortitude, character and honesty as well the one who is arrogant, gluttonous, dishonest, spiteful, should be excluded from royal service.[45] In order to keep them on the right track the smrti-writers forbid them to take bribe. Heavy punishment is prescribed in such

37. Garuda, CXII.
38. Manu, VII. 65.
39. *Ibid.*, VII. 66
40. *Ibid.*, VII. 122
41. Yaj. I. 328.
42. *Ibid.*, I. 338.
43. Manu, VII. 61.
44. Vas. Dh. S. XVI. 22.
45. Garuda, CXII.

cases. Manu advises the king to deprive the Lok Sewaks of their property if they take bribes.[46] He adds that the servants who are appointed to protect the people, general become thieves who seize his subjects against such man.[47] Yajnavalkya too prescribes banishment for the takers of bribes, who according to him should be first deprived of their wealth.[48] Katyayana also voices the same opinion when he says that if a man who is assigned certain duties by the king, obtains a bribe he should be made to return the whole of the money given as bribe and to pay a fine eleven times as much to the king.[49]

The king's servants were allowed to have recreation in their own houses, through various methods. Apastamba in this connection states that assaults of arms, dancing, singing music and the like performances shall be held only in the house of the king's servants.[50]

In Santi Parva we come to know about another privilege of the Lok Sewaks; Lok Sewaks would be given good treatment by the king because in that case he would never be overtaken by calamities.[51]

Our smrti-writers do not mention in clear terms the privileges of the Lok Sewaks though the Yajnavalkya.

Smrti gives some indications. It states that having known through his spies the conduct of those who are office-holders in his kingdom, the king should humor the righteous and punish the opposite.[52] So these officers were given reward for their good and righteous conduct.

---

46. Manu, IX. 237.
47. *Ibid.*, IX. 237.
48. Yaj. I. 339.
49. Kat. 652-53.
50. Ap. Dh. S. II. 10.25.14.
51. SP, 57.26.
52. Yaj. I. 338.

Chapter

5

Vyavahara (Civil Law)

The Katyayana Smrti occupies a very prominent place among the smrtis. His work is remarkable for vividness and richness of detail, especially in relation to the law of procedure or vyavahara. Katyayana represents the high watermark of the smrti rules about procedure and has a great penchant for distinctions and definitions.[1]

Defining vyavahara Katyayana says, "When the ramifications of right conduct, that together are called Dharma and that can be established only with effort, have been violated, the dispute (in a law court between plaintiff and defendant) which springs from what is desired to be proved (such as a debt), is said to be 'vyavahara'." Here 'vi' is employed in the sense of 'various', 'ava' in the sense of 'doubt' and 'hara' means removing of doubts. In plain words the word vyavahara means 'litigation' or a lawsuit. That is said to be vyavahara (decision by judicial proof) where, for the purpose of deciding the causes (of litigants), those who are to execute the secrets law (i.e. the judge and the

1. P.V. Kane, Katyayana Smrti Saroddhar, Int., p. XIV.
2. Kat. 25, 26.
"प्रयत्नसाध्ये विच्छिन्ने धर्मारव्ये न्यायविस्तरे।
साध्यमूलस्तू यो वादों व्यवहारः स उच्चते ।। 25 ।।"

assessors) put forward some principle of Dharmasastras (viz. the examination of plaint, reply, witnesses, etc).

Vyavahara is said to have feet, the plaint, the defense (reply), the deliberations 9 as to the burden of proof) and the adducing of proof.[3] Dharmasastra (sacred law) and Arthasastra are declared to be the two main branches of vyavahara and victory and defeat are declared to be the two fruits.[4] According to Yajnavalkya when a person, oppressed by others in a manner contrary to law and custom, petitions to the king, that becomes a topic of vyavahara.[5] Thus it signifies not law generally but only law on topics, which were justifiable by the king. In ancient India there emerged from the general body of relations and ritual law some rules which formed the basis of adjudication and enforcement by the king. This part of law was called vyavahara, rules of king's justice. Vyavahara consisted of rules not laid down by the command of the kings, but those, which the king was bound to follow in the administration of justice. That constrained not only the subject but equally the king himself.[6] We do not found an impressive number of categories of disputes, which form the subject matter of vyavahara in the earlier smrtis. Nor could it be otherwise. As Maine has pointed out these provinces of jurisprudence must shrink within narrower boundaries, the nearer we make approaches to the infancy of social brotherhood.[7] Different smrtis were compiled at different periods and were required to suit the needs of their times. As the violation of law, both civil and criminal, grew an attracted the attention of the learned men, provisions were made for the time and punishment of these violations under king's justice of vyavahara. This of course does not mean that the categories under vyavahara were the only rules or laws in operation. On the contrary, there existed elaborate rules relating to family law, including marriage,

3. *Ibid.*, 31.
4. *Ibid.*, 32.
5. Yaj. II. 5.
6. N.C. Sen Gupta, Comparative View of Law in Ancient India, SCHI, p. 63.
7. Henry Maine, Ancient Law, p. 368.

sonship, kingship, law of duties of students, rules of inheritance, etc. What is to be noted is that in the beginning the scope of vyavahara as king's justice was narrow and it was enlarged with the development of society.

Apastamba is one of the oldest law-givers. A perusal of the different topics of violation of rules and the punishments prescribed by Apastamba shows that a very limited number of titles have been unclouded in his scheme of vyavahara. These are adultery by the sudras and the three higher castes,[8] abuse, theft and assault[9] by sudras on higher castes, homicide by brahmanas[10] and crime of violation by one of the rules of his caste of order.[11] Morecover, certain violations relate to the productive sector of society, such as the failure on the part of the householder to produce in the land taken on lease, abandoning of work by servants and herdsmen of cattle and trespass by cattle in royal forests.[12] The punishments prescribed for the offence of adultery are discriminatory for member of the first three castes. Banishment is prescribed for adultery with a woman of the sudra caste whereeas for a sudra who commits adultery with a woman of the first three castes capital punishment is provided.[13] Surprisingly enough, for a brahamana committing adultery with a married woman of equal class performance of one-fourth of penance prescribed for an outcaste is prescribed.[14]

It is significant that the jurisdiction of king's justice or vyavahara did not extend to all persons committing one and the same offence of adultery.

Similar rules are found in relation to theft. Apastamba states that the thief should go to the king, confess his guilty and receive a blow with a club;[15] if he dies, his sin is expiated. But he also prescribes other alternative such as

8. Ap. Dh. S. II. 10.27.8-13.
9. *Ibid.*, II.10.27.14-16.
10. *Ibid.*, II.10.27.16-17.
11. *Ibid.*, II.10.27.18-19.
12. *Ibid.*, II.10.28.1-3.
13. *Ibid.*, II.10.27.8-9.
14. *Ibid.*, II.10.27.11.
15. *Ibid.*, I.9.25.4.

throwing himself into the fire, or repeated performing severe austerities,[16] or killing himself by diminishing daily his portion of food,[17] or undergoing rikkhra penances for one year.[18] Here justices at the hands of the king and penances are provided for the same crime of sin. Gautama's topics of vyavahara includes a wide range of titles. Besides the various crimes, insult, assault, theft, damage caused by cattles etc, he introduces such subjects as debt,[19] interest[20] and adverse possession.[21] It appears that with the passage of time economic transactions of different nature such as ending, borrowing, etc. had developed considerably, which necessitated the inclusion of such topics in vyavahara of king's justice. Another significant topic introduced by Gautama relating to adverse possession is that the property other than land and women belonging to a person who is neither an idiot nor a minor, having been to him who use it.[22] In the eyes of Gautama a person in the service of a thief known to him as such,[23] and one who deliberately receives stolen goods are considered accomplices.[24]

Manu enumerates cases falling under eighteen titles of the law, which the king should decide. These are: non-payment of debts; deposits and pledge; sale without ownership, disputes among partners; resumption of gifts; non-payment of wages; dishonouring of agreements; remission of sale and purchase; disputes regarding boundaries; assault; defamations; theft; robbery and violence; adultery; duties of a man and wife; position of inheritance; gambling and betting.[25] These eighteen topics cover both civil and criminal cases. In Manu therefore the number of topics

---

16. *Ibid.*, I.9.25.6.
17. *Ibid.*, I.9.25.17.
18. *Ibid.*, I.9.25.7.
19. Gaunt, Dh. S. XII. 40-42.
20. *Ibid.*, XII. 29-36.
21. *Ibid.*, XII. 37-39.
22. *Ibid.*, VII. 37.
23. *Ibid.*, XII. 49.
24. *Ibid.*, VII. 50.
25. *Ibid.*, VIII. 4-7.

covered by vyavahara greatly increases and they include such topics require subtle distinction and appreciation of civil law. Sale without ownership concerns among partners, resumption of gifts, remission of sale and purchase, non-performance of agreements, partition or inheritance are examples to show that the scope of vyavahara had enlarged greatly by the time of the Manu Smrti. Yajnavalkya Smrti shows that the law of procedure and evidence to be followed in civil disputes had made considerable progress by the fourth c. AD. Vyavaharapada, cause for judicial proceedings, arises if any right of a person is infringed or any wrong is done to him by another in contravention o the smrtis or customary law.[26] The code of Yajanvalkya is the first to work out a definite law of procedure of some detail. It suggests that be the time of the compilation of this code administration of justice by rained practical lawyers had been fully established.[27] The law -books of Narada and Brhaspati show the maturity attained by the legal system, and may well be regarded as treatises on law and procedure. They include a much larger category of legal actions to be covered by vyavahara or king's justice.

Both the Arthasastra of Kautilya and the smrtis emphasize the importance of administering law impartially and justly. The duty of a king consists in protecting his subnets with justice. Only when the king exercises his power *danda* with impartiality and in proportion to the guilt, either over his son or his enemy, he maintains his own position both in this world and in the next.[28] Ends of justice require that the king must punish the guilty.[29] If the fails, the guilt falls in his duty of infliction punishment on the guilty should undergo a penance.[30] In cases a criminal worthy of punishment is allowed to be free, the king shall do penance by fasting,[31] the same would apply to him in the event of an

26. Yaj. II. 5.
27. N.C. Sen, Evolution of Ancient Indian Law, p. 52.
28. AS, BK. III Ch. I.
29. Ap. Dh. S. II. 11.29.13.
30. Vas. Dh. S. XIX.48.
31. *Ibid.*, XIX. 40.

innocent man being punished.[32] If the king pardons a offender,[33] a quarter of the guilt falls on him. Another quarter on the party, a third quarter on the witnesses, and a fourth quarter on the judges.[34] Justice must not be destroyed by injustice and truth by falsehood while the judges work on, for they shall also be destroyed.[35] Upholding justice is of prime importance for "justice being violated, destroys, justice being preserved, preserves, therefore justice must not be violated, lest violated justice destroys us."[36] When engaged in judicial proceedings the king must make strenuous efforts to find out the truth or right in order to impart justice "as a hunter traces the (wounded) deer by the drops of blood."[37] Yajnavalkya says that the king should eschew anger and greed and decide the cases according to the Dharmasastra.[38] He should nominate such persons on the sabha or jury as are well read in the Vedas, know the Darmasastra are truthful and are free from anger and hatred.[39] Yajnavalkya does not have members of tribunals or the judges to suffer sin or guilt alone in the event of their deflecting from justice and impartiality; he advances further and prescribes even imposition of fines of the erring members of tribunals for giving perverted decision influenced by love, freed or fear,[40] A self-restrained king who passes just sentences at trials, obtain religious merit, gain, fame, esteem among men, reverence on the part of his subjects, victories in war and an everlasting residence in paradise.[41]

The king should be equitable towards all beings, discarding selfish interests.[42] If the king is intent on doing his

32. *Ibid.*, XIX. 4.
33. *Ibid.*, XIX. 4.
34. Baud, Dh. S. 1.10.19.8; Manu, VIII. 18.
35. Manu, VIII. 14.
36. *Ibid.*, VIII. 14.
37. *Ibid.*, VII. 45.
38. Yaj. II. 1.
39. *Ibid.*, II. 2.
40. *Ibid.*, II. 4.
41. Nar. I. 32-33. Int.
42. *Ibid.*, I. 34. Int.

duty, he must be particularly anxious to discover what is right and what is wrong.[43] He should examine judicial quarrels between two litigant parties in just manner acting on the principles of equity and discarding both love and hatred.[44] When lawsuit is decided properly, the members of the court are free from guilt. Their purity depends on the justice of the sentences passed by them.[45] Brhaspati explains the importance of justice using the simile of a tree. A brahmana is the root of the tree of justice; the sovereign prince is its stem and branches; just government is its fruit.[46] Here Brhaspati is looking at different elements of justice. Peace and prosperity depend upon justice in society. Therefore, the king should behave in a just way towards the litigants and should give a just verdict discarding avarice and other evil propensities.[47]

As the ancient Indian society established itself, the various political and legal institutions also got established and strengthened. The law based on sacred texts, customs and royal edicts were not stagnant but were developments of a growing society. Crystalisation of four varnas meant a social division of the labour force of the Aryan community, ensuring its economic and social prosperity. Maintenance and preservation of this set-up required that the laws must be enforced. It was essential that members of every varna or jati performed their duties. In cases of violation the culprits should be brought to book. All this could be possible on the basis of confidence in the judicial system of the time. whereby the rulers and the ruled both knew that juṣtice based on truth would be imparted by the king or the courts set-up by him. Administration of justice was necessary to maintain peace and order. It was thought that in the absence of such a judicial system, the society would be engulfed by anarchy and break into pieces. Having defined, enunciated

43. *Ibid.*, I. 68. Int.
44. Quotation from Nar. I. 4.
45. Nar. III. 7. Int.
46. Br. I. 34.
47. Br. I. 36

and laid down the law as suited for the preservation of the social order based on caste system it was necessary that the principles laid down by that law be applied justly and justice imparted on the basis of these laws without fear or favour. Only this could restore confidence in the judicial system an ultimately in the political system of the time, and save the society from chaos and anarchy. The smrti-writers therefore naturally take much pains to ordain and emphasize that the kin or the tribunals appointed by him should decide the cases fairly, without favours and on merits.

Chapter

6

Court (Nyayalaya)

Administration of justice by the king or the other tribunals gradually gained importance. By the fourth and the fifth c. AD complexities of judicial administration required formal institutions of a more specialized type. The king's court became the forum of the adjudication of disputes, civil and criminal, which lay beyond the purview of the lower courts.[1] During the period of the Maurtas court building in the capital was called Dharmasthiyam and was situated near the great building called Magamatriyam. The offices of the ministry and the Imperial High Court were situated in independent blocks. Near the High Court building lay the hall with necessary accessories of the convenience of the judges and the jurymen. The hall was an important place, and it was a public place.[2] The place where the decision of the truth of the plaint (the cause or root of the dispute) was carried on by consideration of the rules of the sacred law was called the Hall of Justice.[3] The hall was called Sabha by Sumati and others.[4] It appears to be an accepted view of the

1. Drekmeir, Kingship and Community in Early India, p. 236.
2. K.P. Jayaswal, Manu and Yajnavalkya, p. 110.
3. Kat. 52.
4. K.P. Jayaswal, Manu and Yajnavalkya, p. 110.

time that the proceedings of the court should not be held in camera. Therefore, the character of the Hall of Justice is based on the principle of publicity.[5] According to Brhaspati the king should build a house with water and trees adjacent to it. It should be constructed in the middle of the fortress and must be separated from other buildings. The king should use one room of this house as a court of justice. The court room must be well furnished with garlands and a throne, supplied with grain, decorated with jewels, adorned with statues, pictures and images of deities and provided with lore and water.[6] The rules of architecture followed in the construction of building for courts kept in view the tropical conditions, and attention was also given to add grandeur to it by various decorations. The law books formed part of the equipment at least during the time of Sumati, who fully emphasizes the value of reading his code.[7]

THE COMPOSITION OF THE COURT

We have noted earlier that many disputes were decided by organized groups, professions and communities which were recognized by the king as courts within their respective jurisdictions. We hear of Kantakasodhana courts within their respective jurisdictions. All offences under their jurisdiction are enumerated separately by the law-giver Sumati.[8] Brhaspati states that each group should settle its cases according to this own rules. He recognizes the existence of several groups with their own organization. Cultivators, artisans (such as carpenters and others), artists, moneylenders, associations of tradesmen, dancers, persons wearing the token of a religious order and even robbers from different groups.[9] Different courts must be provided for persons belonging to different profession. The courts must be formed in those places where they live, for example, for persons roaming the

5. *Ibid.*, p. 110.
6. Br. I. 18-19
7. K.P. Jayaswal, Manu and Yajnavalkya, p. 111.
8. *Ibid.*, p. 117.
9. Br. I. 26.

forest a court should be summoned in the forest; for warriors in the camp; and for merchants in the caravan.[10] Thus the different guilds of artisans, merchants, etc. can administer their own affairs according to their own laws and customs. Such a provision must have an additional advantage of keeping the courts in the midst of the people and preventing the emergence of gulf between them which more often than not causes miscarriage of justice. Different associations such as meetings of the kindred, companies and artisans, assemblies of cohabitants and the chief judge the right to appeal in succession.[11] This local participation in the administration of justice introduced a democratic element in these tribunals.

Brhaspati classified the courts in the country into four categories: (i) stationary, (ii) not stationary, (iii) furnished with the king's signet ring, and (iv) directed by the king.[12] A stationary court meets in a town or a village, the itinerant court is movable and held at different places with the king's signet ring or the royal seal, is superintended by the chief judge, and one directed by the king is held in the king's prudence.[13] It is indeed interesting to find on the one hand courts manned by the groups, professions, etc. themselves and on the other groups, professions, etc. Themselves, and on the other movable courts which must render them altogether stranger to the condition of the areas they visited.

It is difficult to find out the exact purpose of having movable courts. Probably such courts were devised to meet the emergency of the breakdown of law and order in a particular locality or they were meant to hold summary trials of certain sections of criminals. According to Katyayana family, council, corporations, assemblies, appointed judges and the king held the responsibility of deciding disputes. Of these each one succeeding is superior to the one, which proceeds.[14]

10. *Ibid.*, I. 25.
11. Br. I. 29.
12. *Ibid.* I. 2.
13. Br. I. 3.
14. Kat. 82.

Courts were generally formed on a hierarchal basis. If inferior courts failed to dispose of the cases the superior courts had the jurisdiction to hear the case and give their verdict. If a case was not adequately investigated by the meetings of kindered, it was to be decided after due deliberations by companies of artisans. If it was not duly examined by companies of artisans, it was to be decided by assemblies of co-habitants, and if it was not sufficiently judged by such assemblies of co-habitants, and if it was not sufficiently judged by such assemblies; it was to be tried by the appointed judge.[15] An assembly consisting of at least ten members should decide disputed points of law when the sistas (learned) have failed to do so.[16] Four men who each know of the four Vedas, a mimamsaka one who knows the Angas, one who recited the works on the sacred law, and them brahmanas belonging to three different orders constitute an assembly, consisting at least of ten members.[17] Brhaspati equates a judicial assembly in sanctity to a sacrificial meeting in which sit seven or five or three brahmanas, who are acquainted with the world, with the contents of the Veda, and with law.[18] He does not explain the reasons for ensuing dominance of the brahmanas in the judicial assembly. Of course, as the law books are compiled by the brahmanas they claim a high place of themselves in the judicial organization. However, a separate class of brahmanas was entrusted with the judicial duty.

The smrti-writers, however, emphasize the need to have only knowledgeable brahmanas on the judicial assemblies. In their opinion even thousands of brahmanas cannot form a legal assembly for declaring the sacred law, if they do not fulfil their sacred duties, are not acquainted with the Veda, and subsist only by the name of their caste.[19] Narada also analyses certain features of the judicial assembly.

15. Br. I. 30.
16. Baud, Dh. S. 1.1.1.7.
17. *Ibid.*, 1.1.1.18.
18. Br. I. 11.
19. Baud, Dh. S. 1.1.1.16; Vas, Dh. S. III.5.

"That is not a judicial assembly where there are no elders. They are not elders who do not pass a just sentence. That is not a just sentence in which there is no truth. That is not truth which is vitiated by error."[20] It cannot be said with certainty whether by using the term 'elder'. Narada seeks to prescribe a minimum age limit for qualifying to become a member of the judicial assembly. In some contexts 'elder' might mean also one who is mature in learning and in knowledge of the Vedas or in following his duties properly. It is the duty of the chief judge to 'extract' the dart of inequity from the law-suit, but it is only when the whole aggregate of the members of a judicial assembly declare it to be right that the law-suit loses the dart otherwise the dart remains in it.[21]

According to Narada there are eight members of a court. These are the king, his dutiful officer, the assessors of the court, the logbook, the accountant and scribe, gold, fire and water.[22] A verse attributed to Brhaspati runs thus: "the chief judge publishes the sentence. The king passes it. The assessors investigate the fact of the case, the logbook dictates the judgment, i.e. the victory of the one party and the fine imposed on the other party. Gold and silver serve the purpose by administering ordeals. Water is used for relieving thirst or appeasing hunger. The accountant has to compute the sums. The scribe has to record the proceedings. The attendant must compel the defendant and the witnesses to appear in court, and detain the plaintiff and defendant, if they give no sureties."[23]

The assessors or judges investigated the truth or otherwise involved in a case, and it was their duty to see that the verdict of the court does not deflect from truth and justice. If the assessors of the court realize that the king is becoming undutiful, they should not give such decisions as are agreeable to the king. Instead they should proclaim

---

20. Baud. Dh. S. 1.1.1.16; Vas, Dh. S. III.
21. Nar. III. 16-17. Int.
22. *Ibid.*, I. 15. int.
23. Quoted by Julius Jolly, SBE, Vol. XXXIII, Part I, p. 8, fn. Br. I. 6-9.

justice, which would free them from all sins or the injustices.[24] Katyayana declares that when a member of the court finds the mind of the king is straying from the path of justice, he should them say what is not agreeable to the king; by doing so the Sabhya would not incur sin. Here again a member of the court must speak out words that are in accordance with the sacred law and the science of statecraft. If the king does not listen to the advice of the Sabhya the latter would then be free from sin.[25] In the event of the king directing the members of the court to give a wrong or unjust, decision, a member of the court should explain to the king that royal order will lead to injustice, so that the king is turned away from wrong doing.[26] It appears that assessors were chosen from amongst the ranks or the class of the disputants; for example, it was laid that the assessor would be a gambler if the dispute arises out of the games.[27] In the event of verdict being contrary to justice, the assessors of the court must pay a fine, because nobody certainly an act as a judge without incurring the risk of being punished eventually.[28]

A number of qualifications are prescribed for the accountant on the scribe. They should possess certain qualification such as thorough familiarity with grammar and vocabulary, skill in the art of computation, honesty and acquaintance with various mode of writing.[29] If the court clerk does not take down what has been deposed by the parties, enters what has not been deposed, or records evidence in an ambiguous manner he is liable to punishment.[30]

Stobhaka and Sucaka are to be appointed for detecting the crimes. The Stobhaka is defined as one who with the sole

24. Kat. 76.
25. Kat. 77.
26. *Ibid.*, 78.
27. Yaj. III. 203.
28. Nar. I. 66. Int.
29. Br. I. 14.
30. Kat. 132.

eye to money and without being urged by the king first informs the king of matter which is censored by the sastras.[31] A Sucaka is to be appointed by the king himself for discovering the wrong doing of others and for conveying this information.[32] However, a person acquainted with law could give his opinion even if he was not an authorized person.[33] Katyayana adopts a very clear attitude and declares that whatever is done by others as judges must be regarded as done wrongly, even if such persons are officers of the king and even if the decision is according to the sacred texts, it has to be declared null and void.[34] Here we have an example of the separation of the judicial wing of administration from the executive and it is sought to be effected by declaring all judgments-giver by persons other than judicial officers without jurisdiction and as such illegal and unenforceable.

KING'S COURT

The smrtis give a clear idea of royal court. The king Agter having completed his morning routine, and having shown due respect to his guru, astrologer, physicians, deities, brahmanas and the family priests, should enter the courtroom with a pleasing appearance.[35] He should be dressed in a simple manner. After reaching the courtroom with a composed mind, together with persons learned in the three Vedas, elders and counselors well versed in statecraft he should look into the causes of litigants.[36] He should decide the causes in the courtroom in the first half of the day according to the course laid down in the sastras.[37] The three parts of the day after the first eighth part are recognized in the sastras by the wise as the time of administration of

31. Kat. 33.
32. Kat. 34.
33. *Ibid.*, III. 2.
34. Kat. 68.
35. Kat. 53-54
36. *Ibid.*, 55.
37. *Ibid.*, 60.

justice.[38] According to Brhaspati the king accompanied by elders, ministers and attendants should not attend the court only in the morning but also in the afternoon.[39] He should always listen to the exposition of the puranas, codes of law and the rules of polity.[40] The king must occupy the seat of justice. He should be covered with clothes and he should state the trial of causes with a cool and collected mind. Cases must be decided according to the order of the caste.[41] A king desirous on investigating the lawsuits must enter his court of justice preserving a dignified demeanor, together with the brahmanas and the experienced counselors.[42] According to Yajnavalkya the king divested of anger and avarice associated with learned brahmanas should investigate the judicial proceedings according to the sacred code of laws.[43] He should face the east, the judges the north, the accountant the west and his scribe the south.[44] Assistance to the king by his employees through the discharge of their duties was important. In the opinion of a lawgiver a king will be superior even to a brahamana if he lives surrounded by servants who are keen eyed like vultures.[45] But if he is surrounded by servants who are greedy like[46] vultures he will not be exalted. Therefore, first instruction is emphasized in his case.[47]

Preservation of justice was essential to avoid destruction. The king is guilty if he does not inflict punishment on the criminal. If the king and judges impart justice they are free from sin.[48] It is the king's duty to keep members of the judiciary actuated by wrath, ignorance or covetousness has passed an unjust sentence he shall be

38. *Ibid.*, 62.
39. Br. I. 23.
40. *Ibid.*
41. Manu, VIII. 24.
42. *Ibid.*, VIII. 1.
43. Yaj. II. 1.
44. Br. 1.16.
45. Vas. Dh. S. XVI. 21.
46. *Ibid.*, XVI. 22.
47. *Ibid.*, XVI. 23.
48. Manu, VIII. 14.

declared unworthy of the membership of the court, and the king shall punish him for his offence.[49] The king is the appointing (Manu, VIII. 23). authority for the judges of the court. He is advised to appoint those who are honourable, men of tried integrity and able to bear the burden of administration of justice.[50] A veracious man, who obeys the king, should be appointed by him as his own officer to summon and to keep in custody the witnesses, plaintiff and defendant.[51] The king can delegate some judicial duties to the different associations. Relatives, companies of artisans, assemblies of cohabitants and other persons, if they are authorized by the king, enjoy the jurisdictions to decide the lawsuits excepting those concerning violent crimes.[52] If the king is absent on account of some reasons, he should appoint a learned brahmana to try the cases. Such an appointed person shall not decide the case independently but together with three assessors.[53]

Certain cases fall outside the purview of the royal jurisdiction. The disputes of ascetics and of persons versed in sorcery and witchcraft are to be settled by persons familiar with the three Vedas only. The king should not settle their disputes for fear of rousing their resentment.[54]

Impartiality is considered to be essential for the administration of justice. The king is asked not to be partial to one of the two parties involved in a dispute.[55] He has to reason properly regarding an offence, which will finally be determined as a result of this process. One, who properly examined an offence in accordance with the sum of the science of the first two castes, is equitable towards all created beings.[56] Here the expression "according to the sum of the science of the first two castes" means according to the rules

49. Nar. I. 67. Int.
50. *Ibid.*, III. 4.
51. Br. I. 15.
52. *Ibid.*, I. 28.
53. Manu, VIII. 9-10; Kat. 63-64.
54. Br. I. 27; Kat. 83.
55. Vas. Dh. S. XVI. 3.
56. Vas. Dh. S. XVI. 5.

of sacred learning and of the mimamsa which is peculiar to the brahmanas, and of logic (anviksiki) and polity (dandaniti) which are peculiar to the Ksatriyas.[57] The "sum of the science" of the two superior ruling castes was supposed to be equitable towards all created being, including the Vaisyas and Sudras, who were the toiling and exploited sections in society. In this sense, the fundamental approach of ancient Indian lawgivers towards law and justice was partisan. It was essentially based on the ideas and concepts held by the privileged class, who claimed that whatever suited them must also suit all the other created beings.

Narada says that the king must be impartial. He should not be actuated by arrogance of avarice not promote litigation among persons not engaged in a controversy.[58] He shall investigate judicial proceedings in a bonafide manner rejecting ambiguity.[59] In deciding cases, he should take into consideration the dictates of the law book and should hear the opinion of his chief judge.[60] He should try the cases in due order exhibiting great care.[61] Where the rules of sacred law and the dictates of prudence are at variance, he must discard the first in favour of the second.[62] When it is impossible to act up to the precepts of sacred law, it becomes necessary to adopt a method founded on reasoning because "custom decides everything and over rules the sacred law."[63] Here the king is definitely advised to respect the immemorial usages and customs of every province and not to overrule them even if the sacred law is contrary to them. Vasistha and Gautama also prescribe the method of proper reasoning so that the offence will become evident finally.[64] Katyayana holds that in all disputes the king should always give a decision by means of the pramanas (documents, witnesses, possession) or by inference or even by ordeals.

57. Buhleer, SBE, Vol. XIV, Part II, p. 79 n.
58. Quotations from Nar. I. 3-4.
59. Yaj. II. 19.
60. Nar. I. 35. Int.
61. *Ibid.*, I. f 35.
62. *Ibid.*, I. 39.
63. *Ibid.*, I. 40.
64. Vas. Dh. S. XVI. 4; Gaut, Dh. S. XI. 23.

JUDGES (NYAYADHEESH)

Judges played an important role in the administration of justice with the growth in the number of disputes as also the preoccupation of the king with mounting problems and duties of non-judicial nature. For deciding the suits it was natural, therefore to place more reliance on the judges who must have gained importance accordingly.[65]

The accepted idea of the period was that the brahmanas were not to be judged by one who was not at least their equal. Secondly, science the suit involved in the crime must also be legally examined, judges had to be drawn from the guardians and interpreters of Dharma.[66] Under the code of Manu, brahmanas were given the right to claim judgeship which is contrary to the previous history. This applied, however, only to the Civil Court; Kantakasodhana (Criminal Courts) were not presided over by them.[67]

The smrti-kars invariably emphasize that only qualified brahmanas should be appointed is a brahmana by caste, for that the judge to be appointed is a brahmana by caste, for what four or even three brahmanas well read in the Vedas proclaim is distinctly recognized as the sacred law and not the decision of a thousand fools.[68] Narada states that the brahmana had the privilege to become the chief judge but adds that he should be thoroughly well read in the Vedas and Vedangas, instructed in sacred learning and religious conduct, tranquil-minded and unambitious.[69] Further, he is required to be truthful, pure able and delighting in the welfare of all sentient beings.[70] The chief judge or the pradvivaka should be fully acquainted with the eighteen titles of law and the eight thousand sub-division thereof, be skilled in logic and other branches of science and thoroughly versed

65. Kat. 241.
66. Drekmeir, Kingship and Community in Early India, p. 235.
67. K.P. Jayaswal, Manu and Yajnavalkya, p. 71.
68. Vas. Dh. S. III. 7.
69. Quotations from Nar. VI. 17.
70. *Ibid.*, VI. 18.

in revealed and traditional lore.[71] The court should be presided over by incorruptible and diligent assessors, by wise brahmansa who are hereditary, who are well versed in the meaning of sacred texts and the science of politics. Katyayana also includes among the assessors a few merchants who form a group or guild, who are men of high family of character, elderly in age, are endowed with good conduct and wealth and are free from malice; they are to be appointed to listen to the cause and to look to the administration of justice.[72] Katyayana says that where a brahmana endowed with these qualities cannot be had, the king should appoint a Ksatriya or a Vaisya proficient in the sacred law; but he (the king) should carefully avoid a Sudra as judge.[73] The chief judge should investigate the law relating to the case in hand by putting questions on passing divisions (vivekayati) according to what was heard or understood by him.[74] Brhaspati prescribes certain qualifications for the judges such as ability to perform the devotional acts, qualifications of being strictly veracious and virtuous, of being void of wrath and covetousness and of being familiar with the legal lore.[75] According to Katyayana, the courtroom should include a Ksatriya or Vaisya proficient in the sacred law. The king should, however, carefully avoid a Sudra as a judge.[76] This is significant in many respects. Inclusion of merchants or Vaisyas might reflect the growing importance of trade and possibly wealth in the social order of the time. The merchants generally and some merchants particularly must have gathered enough wealth and economic importance to enable their entrance into the courts, which was all along a coveted privilege of the brahmanas. The position has changed very significantly. It is no longer necessary that an assessor of the court should be a brahmanas in the past. On the contrary, it is prescribed that assessors should be such brahmanas as are not avaricious, know the

71. Quotations from Nar. I. 1-2.
72. Kat. 57-59.
73. *Ibid.*, 67.
74. Quotation from Nar. I. 1-2.
75. Br. I. 13. Yaj. II. 2.
76. Kat. 67.

sacred law, as always speak the truth and are proficient in all Sastras but have also the additional qualification of possessing wealth.[77]

Certain persons are declared to be disqualified from being consulted in the decision of a case. They include those who are ignorant of the customs of the country, are unbelievers, despisers of the scared books, insane, irate, avaricious or troubled by pain or illness.[78] These qualifications underline once again the respect for customs and usages. They also indicate the complete exclusion of the followers of the non-conformist religions and philosophies. The rulers and sages probably believed that only by keeping such elements out of the administration of justice the existence of the Aryan society, its social and economic order, could be preserved.

JUDGES AND THEIR DUTIES

The brahmana who was the chief judge, used to inflict the punishment of gentle admonition and harsh reproof. The king could impose both fines and corporal punishment.[79] Either the king or any member of a twice-corn caste officiating as chief judge should try a cause.[80] But they were required to observe the principles of equity, the opinion of the majority of the judges and the doctrine of the sacred law.[81] The liability of the judges to incur sin in the event of the passing of an unjust verdict is emphasized again and again.[82] Where the sabhyas decide a matter in violation of the sacred laws justice is overcome by injustice. It undoubtedly destroys the king.[83] The sabhyas (assessors) are themselves destroyed where justice is slain by injustice, and truth is strangled by untruth while the assessors look on with

77. Kat. 71.
78. Br. I. 33.
79. Br. XXVII. 8.
80. *Ibid.,* I. 24.
81. *Ibid.,* I. 24.
82. Caut, Dh. S. XIIL 11; Baud, Dh. S. 1.10.19.8; Nar. III. 10-12
83. Kat. 72.

apathy.[84] The preservation of justice and truth is considered to be of such paramount importance that the members of the court were asked not to connive even with the king when he begins to act unjustly. If they do so, they along with the king fall headlong into the hell.[85] The assessors are instructed to advise the king to follow the path of righteousness.[86] Yajnavalkaya expects the sabhyas to be impartial, and in order to ensure such a conduct he prescribes fine for those who due to love, greed or fear go against the rules of the Dharmasastras.[87] Visnu prescribes heavy fine against corrupt judges and even the confiscation of their entire property.[88] The importance of a verdict given impartially and without being influenced by extraneous factors was fully appreciated and underlined. Katyayana lies down that if the judges were to hold conversation in private with a party while the matter in dispute is undecided, they become liable to be punished. This applies also to the assessors if they do the same.[89]

The duty of the chief judge was to superintend the whole of the proceedings of the ordeal. He must fast and obey the king's instructions in the same way as an Adhvaryu priest officiates at a sacrifice.[90] The judge is enjoined to examine the plaint in question and answer. He should speak gently inspite of the controversy involved.[91] Appointed judges are superior in authority to the other associations; the chief judge ranks above all because he passes the just sentences.[92]

JUDICIAL PROCEDURE

Narada points out that the judicial proceeding has four feet, four bases and four means. It benefits four, reaches four

84. *Ibid.*, 73.
85. *Ibid.* 74.
86. *Ibid.*, 75.
87. Yaj. II. 4. Br. XXII. 10.
88. Visnu, V. 180.
89. Kat. 70.
90. Quotations from Nar. VI. 16.
91. Br. I. 12.
92. *Ibid.*

and produces four results.[93] Virtue, judicial proceedings, documentary evidence and royal edicts are the four feet of a law suit and each following one is superior to the one previously named.[94] Here virtue is based on truth, judicial proceedings rest on the statements of the witnesses, documentary evidence consists of declarations reduced to writings, and an edict depends on the pleasure of the king. Similarly there are four parts of a trial. First, the connection (agama) must be examined, second, the title must be ascertained, third, the case, and at the end a decision is to be given.[95] Because the four means of conciliation and the rest are adopted, it is said to have four means and since judicial procedure protects the four orders. It is said to benefit four.[96] The four results of judicial proceedings are justice, gain, renown and esteem.[97] Because a judicial procedure affects criminals, witnesses, the assessors of the court, and the king to the amount of one quarter each, it is said to reach four.[98] There are four parts of judicial proceedings such as declaration, answer, trial, and deliberation of judges regarding the onusprobandi. Narada's doctrine of 'four' relating to judicial proceedings gives us a fairly good idea of the aspects involved in judicial proceedings in ancient India as also the considerable importance acquired by the law suits in those days. Narada emphasizes the importance of the substance by stating that if the month of the law suits is in order, the whole suit is in order, but not otherwise.[99] Lawsuits are based on the statements of the two litigants. The accusation is called the plaint and the answer the declaration of the defendant.[100] The plaintiff should affirm his case first and then the defendant. When they have finished the

93. *Ibid.*
94. *Ibid.*
95. *Ibid.*
96. *Ibid.*
97. *Ibid.*
98. *Ibid.*
99. *Ibid.*, I. 44.
100. *Ibid.*, I. 28.

members of the court (sabhyas) and after them the judge should speak.[101] The suitor stood before the court bowing the judge asked: "What is thy business? What is thy grievance? Fear not! Speak out, O Man."[102]

If the cause be judicially entertainable the judge should deliver the court seat the plaintiff for calling the defendant or he should order the court officer to call the defendant.[103] The lawsuit could proceed further only when the court was convinced that a *prima facie* case was established by the plaintiff and it was entertainable judicially.

An officer of the court was to reduce to writing the statements of each party, and also whatever else has been written on the board, together with the names of the witnesses as well as the statements in which both parties concur.[104] Even such things as the statement of the plaintiff made under the influence of any of the passions or lust was to be reduced to writing.[105] Accuracy in recording those statements is important, and the scribe who writes down the words of the plaintiff or the defendant differently from what they narrate is to be punished as a thief by the king who desires to enforce Dharma.[106] The additional statements of the plaintiff or defendant which are not contained in the wittings of both the parties are to be subsequently entered into their declaration. These are called pratyakalita, i.e. what is interposed.[107]

If the plaintiff and defendant come into conflict claiming their own superiority or precedence, their declaration is to be received in the order of their castes, or after considering their grievances.[108] Thus the courts too were

---

101. Kat. 121.
102. K.P. Jayaswal, Manu and Yajanvalkya, pp. 121; 86-88.
     काले कार्यार्थिनं यच्छेत प्रजतं पुरतः स्थितम।
     किं कार्यं काचष्ते पीडा मा भैषीब्रूहि मानवः ।। 86 ।।
103. Kat. 87-88.
104. Nar. II. 20.
105. Kat. 129.
106. Kat. 132.
107. Nar. II. 21.
108. Br. III. 4.

permeated in their practice and procedure with caste distinctions and privileges, which clearly shows that the principle of equality before law was not applied even in matters of procedure. This conclusion is strengthened by Narada's view that Sudra has no right to proffer a false accusation against a member of the twice born caste, and if he does so his tongue shall be slit by the officers of the king and he shall be put on the stakes. In similar cases brahmanas are placed above everything.[109]

If a litigant, even when he has been asked to speak out, does not say anything, he deserves to be confined once to the jail and is supposed to be the losing party.[110] Even if the defendant does not present himself when a decision is to be taken on usages, a gift of money, desirable actions and services, the king should not cause an error in decision by deciding in the defendant's absence.[111]

The principle that judgments should not be passed in the absence of the parties seems to have been followed by the court. The impartiality of the verdict is sought to be maintained by the rule that where a litigant induces even a single member of the court to be partial towards him or where he offers a bribe, even to the opponent, he should be treated as a losing party to the dispute.[112] In a civil dispute if a litigant himself threatens the other side or offers a bribe to him or gets him threatened or restrained through another person, he becomes hina, i.e. losing party.[113]

In case where property or money is involved the king should not allow a litigant to proceed with the case. If he retains the property or money which he has been shown to have seized. If he should be delivered over to the other litigant or should be kept with a third person as receiver.[114] It appears that the courts also acted as custodian of properties

109. Nar. II. 37. Int.
110. Kat. 200.
111. *Ibid.*, 160.
112. *Ibid.*, 204.
113. *Ibid.*, 205.
114. *Ibid.* 205.

in disputes during the pendency of the su... Any property either movable or immovable thus kept under the care of the judge, must be returned to the winning party together with the interest accruing over it.[115]

There appears to be a realization that causes should be decided without delay and parties should not be permitted to absent themselves from a providing information and thus cause delay in decisions. Katyayana lays down that if a litigant does not present himself before the court after he is summoned, he loses his cause at once.[116] Similarly where a litigant desires to obtain more time or adjournment merely under a pretext, he should be regarded as deceitful and such conduct be declared to be a reason leading to the loss of the cause to him.[117] The ancient legal procedure provided also for a fresh trial of the cause if a man lost his case through the dishonesty of witnesses or judges. But if he lost the case through his own conduct the trial could not be renewed.[118] According to Katyayana a retrial of the case is allowed to him who has been defeated in accordance with texts speaking of hina' (losing or cast off) litigant. There is, however, no retrial for him who is defeated in accordance with texts that lay down expressly the loss of the matter in dispute.[119] According to Narada, however a case could be tried once more if man was of the opinion that the suit had been decided and punishment declared against him, in contravention to justice, provided he should pay twice the amount of the fine inflicted.[120] A retrial of case is also provided of judgment has not been given in a proper way, i.e. if the law has been judged without any previous examination of witnesses or other evidence, or when it has been decide in an improper manner, or when it has been judged by unauthorized persons.[121]

115. Nar. KP. 15.
116. Kat. 199.
117. *Ibid.*, 201.
118. Nar. II. 40. Int.
119. Kat. 208.
120. Nar. I. 65.
121. *Ibid.*, I. 14.

We come across various kings of tribunals dispensing justice to the citizens such as assemblies of town dwellers, companies of traders and families. These are classified according to their relative importance in the investigation of the affairs of man.[122] An appeal may be preferred from the decision of a family upwards to persons specially appointed by the ruler.[123] The king shall reverse the cases decided by compulsion, by fear, by women, at night inside a house, abroad, and brought forward by enemies.[124]

According to Narada proceedings at law are of two kinds, one, which is not attended by a wager, and the second when either of the two parties stakes in writing a certain sum to be paid, besides the amount in dispute, in case of defeat.[125] If the claim be attended by wager, the losing party is to be compelled to pay a fine, his wager and the thing claimed to the plaintiff.[126] Giving of sureties by the litigant is also prescribed. If there be no surety given by the plaintiff, who has a proper cause for dispute, he is to be guarded and he has to give to the messenger guarding him his wages at the end of the day.[127]

In the event of failure on the part of the person belonging to the three higher castes, he is to be guarded by warders outside the lock up. But the Sudras and others are to be confined and fettered if they cannot give sureties.[128] If the person without surety breaks the restraint put on him and runs away, he is to be fined eight panas. It is, however, prescribed that persons of all castes should not be obstructed in performing their daily obligatory rites or duties such as bathing, worshipping, sandhya prayers, etc.[129]

The courts would not accept everybody as surety. The master, and enemy, or a person who is under arrest and

---

122. Yaj. II. 30.
123. *Ibid.*, II. 31.
124. *Ibid.*, II. 32.
125. Nar. I. 4. Int.
126. Yaj. II. 18.
127. Kat. 117.
128. *Ibid.*, 118.
129. *Ibid.*, 119.

fined, certain categories of accused persons, one appointed on the king's business, ascetics and some others could not be accepted a sureties.[130] According to Yajnavalkya a competent surety must be taken from both parties for the satisfaction of the award.[131] Strangers are not permitted to speak on behalf of others and are to be fined if they do so. Brother, father, son or appointed agent, however, appear to have been permitted to speak on behalf of their litigant relations.'[132] Claimants and defendants can appoint their own representatives who can speak on their behalf in the court. But the victory or defeat would affect the party himself and not the representative.[133] If the defendant puts forward a person other than himself before the judge as defendant the latter should be regarded as the defendant; this also applies if a person is accepted as the defendant by the plaintiff. It is the right of the person charged to give reply and not of another person, since the latter is unconnected with the dispute; but even a stranger may be allowed to have the right to defend if he is put forward as the defendant by the person charged by the plaintiff.[134] A representative of the Plaintiff or the defendant is not allowed in cases involving murder of a brahmana, drinking of wine, theft, indecent assault on another's wife, eating of forbidden food, kidnapping of a maiden and intercourse with her, counterfeiting coins, measures, etc. In such cases the man himself should engage in the dispute.[135]

Certain persons are exempted from personal appearance in the court and allowed to send their representatives. These include idiots, madman, very old people, women, boys or sick persons, for all of whom their kinsmen or appointed agents are to give answers in the court.[136] It appears that in a dispute of criminal nature no

130. *Ibid.*, 114-116.
131. Yaj. II. 10.
132. Nar. P. 23; Kat. 92.
133. Nar. I. 22.
134. Kat. 89-90.
135. Nar. II. 34.
136. P.V. Kane, HDS, Vol. III, p. 294.

court fees are required to be paid. The person found guilty has to pay the king the fine declared in the smrtis for offences.[137] In civil disputed also nothing is paid as court fees at the inception of the suit. Certain rules of course do prescribe payments to the king, but this has to be done after the decision of the suit. Such payments essentially partake the nature of court fees.

137. Kat. III. 1; Yaj. II. 10; Nar. IV. 32; Manu, VIII. 59.

PART II

Chapter

7

Crime and Punishment

The smrtis prescribe various crimes relating to punishments to be awarded for different crimes. Abuse and defamation constituted an important crime, and may have originated frequently from prejudices based on castes for the smrtis lay down punishments for offenders according to his caste. Narada's definition of vǎkparusya also points to such a conclusion. He defines it as abusive speech couched in offensive and violent terms regarding the native country, cast, family of a man, etc.[1] "The Gaudas are quarrelsome", "Brahmanas are extremely greedy", "persons of Visvamitra gotra commit cruel deeds", are a few examples of abuse of country, caste and family respectively.[2]

The nature of punishment as well as the degree prescribed in the smrtis appear to have the objective of preventing acrimony based on caste and other prejudices and to maintain the social position of castes as laid down in the Vedas and smrtis. Gautama states that a Sudra, who intentionally reviles by criminal abuse or assault a member of the twice born caste, is to be deprived of the limb with which

1. Mar, XV. 1.
2. P.V. Kanr. HDS, Vol. III, p. 511.

he offends.[3] Through punishments the sudras are sought to be excluded from learning the Vedas. If he listens to recitations of the Vedas intentionally, his ears are to be filled with molten tin or lac.[4] If he dares to recite the vedic texts his body is to be split.[5] For assuming equal position with members of the upper castes, corporal punishment is prescribed.[6] The anxiety of the smrtis to preserve the varying social status of different castes is reflected also in the rules, which prescribe different punishments for one and the same offence if they are committed by members of different castes. Thus if a ksatriya abuses a brahmanahe is to pay a fine of hundred karsaplanas, but in cases of a brahmana abusing a ksatriya only fifty, a vaisya only twenty-five and nothing in the case of a sudra.[7] For a sudra Visnu prescribes a fine of twelve panas for abusing a man of one's own caste.[8] For abusing a member of lower castes the fine is only six panas.[9] If a kastriya defames a brahmana he is to pay a fine of one hundred panas, but in the cases of a vaisya the fine prescribed is one hundred and fifty or two hundred panas. If a sudra does it corporal punishment is to be inflicted.[10] When a brahmana defames a ksatriya he is to pay a fine of fifty panas, but in the case of defaming a vaisya and sudra a fine of only twenty-five and twelve panas respectively.[11] The fact that Manu makes abusing a sudra punishable with a fine of twelve panas whereas Gautama prescribes nothing (Gaut. Dh. S. XII. 13-14) shows that during the time of Manu sudra's position improved somewhat in this respect. Visnu also prescribes a fine of the first amercement for insulting a sudra.[12] At the same time Manu appears to be very stern and

3. Gaut. Dh. S. XII. 1. Ap. Dh. S. II. 10.27.14. Manu, VIII. 270, 279-83.
4. Gaut. Dh. S. XII. 4.
5. *Ibid.* XII. 5.
6. *Ibid.*, XXI. 6.
7. *Ibid.*, XII. 8-13; AS, BK. III. Ch. XVIII.
8. Visnu, V 35.
9. *Ibid.*, V. 36
10. Manu, VIII. 267; Nar. XV-XVI. 15.
11. Manu, VIII. 268l Nar. XV-XVI. 16; Br. XX. 7.
12. Visnu, V. 103.

hard in dealing with the offences in which a twice born man is insulted by a sudra; he prescribes cutting out of the tongue[13] and thrusting into his mouth of red hot iron nail.[14] According to Manu if the sudra has the arrogance to teach brahamanas then should see that hot oil is poured into his mouth and into his ears.[15] The same is prescribed by Visnu when a low born man mentions the name or caste of a superior revealingly.[16] The underlying principle behind the above discriminatory rule appears to be that men of high social position must be protected against low persons and such low person insulting a brahamana must be awarded severe punishment. Brhasapati states that person begotten in the inverse order of caste and members of the lowest caste are called the refuse of society; if they insult a brahmana they must be corporally punished and must never be amerced in a fine.[17]

It is abvious that the nature and degree of punishments prescribed in the smrtis is discriminatory, and the discrimination itself is frankly justified. It has two dimensions. First, it is based on the caste of the person who commits the offence. Secondly, it is based on the caste of the victim of such an offence. The combined objective of the whole provision is to preserve and enforce the system and caste inequalities with the help of the coercive powers and machinery of the state.

The Arthasastra of Kautilya states that when a ksatriya commits adultery on an unguarded brahmana woman a fine of the highest amercement is to be awarded. In case of a vaisya his entire property is to be confiscated; but a sudra is to be burnt alive.[18] Where a man commits adultery with a woman of low caste he is to be put to death.[19] When a sudra

13. Manu, VIII. 270.
14. *Ibid.*, VIII. 271.
15. *Ibid.*, VIII. 272; Nar. XV-XVI.24.
16. Visnu, V. 25, Nar. XV-XVI.23.
17. Br. XXI. 15.
18. AS, Bk. IV. Ch. XIII.
19. *Ibid.*, Bk. IV. Ch. XIII.

approaches a woman of brahmana caste he is to be burnt alive.[20] When a vaisya and ksatriya approach a woman of the brahmana caste they are to be burnt.[21] Similarly when a vaisysa offends a ksatriya woman, he is to be burnt.[22] In class involving adultery between a man of a twice born caste with a woman of the sudra caste the man is to be banished.[23] But a sudra committing the same offence with a woman of the first three castes, must suffer capital punishment.[24] In contrast to all these, where a brahmana commits adultery once with a married woman of equal class the needs only to perform one-fourth of the penance prescribed for an out caste.[25]

Punishment for offences relating to sex is not confined to only cases in which married women are involved but also covers criminal intercourse with women in general. If a man has criminal intercourse with an Aryan woman his organ is to be cut off, and all his property confiscated.[26] Ápastamba prescribes for adultery the cutting of the organ of the adulterer but introduces a distinction in the crime of intercourse with a marriageable girl by providing the punishment of confiscation of property and banishment of the adulterer.[27] Manu recommends cutting of two fingers of the man forcibly contaminating a maiden besides making his pay six hundred panas as fine.[28] In the case of a man of equal caste defiling a willing maiden only a fine of two hundred panas is prescribed in order to deter him from repetition of the offence.[29] If however, a sudra has intercourse with a woman of a twice born caste punishment of loss of part and confiscation of property and even loss of life is provided.[30]

20. Vas. Dh. S. XXI. 1; Gaiut. Dh. S. XXIII 15.
21. *Ibid.*, XXI. 23.
22. *Ibid.*, XXI. 4-5.
23. Ap. Dh. S. II. 10.27.8.
24. *Ibid.*, II. 10.27.9; Manu, VIII. 374; Yaj. II. 86.
25. Ap. Dh. S. II. 10.27.11.
26. Gaut. Dh. S. XII. 2.
27. Ap. Dh. S. II. 10.26.20.
28. Manu, VIII. 367.
29. *Ibid.*, VIII. 368.
30. *Ibid.*, VIII. 374.

According to Narada when a man has connections with a woman of his own caste a fine of the highest degree is prescribed, but when this involves a woman of lower caste the middling fine is prescribed, In case he has connections with a woman of superior caste capital punishment is to be awarded.[31]

Narada also draws a distinction between connection of a man with a willing woman; he prescribes severe punishment including death and confiscation of entire property in the later case if the woman belongs to the brahmana caste.[32]

Smrti laws seem to have appreciated clearly the difference in the nature and gravity of sexual crimes involving woman belonging to another man (married woman adultery) and unwilling woman and a willing woman. Connections with a woman who is not one's wife (excepting certain categories of fallen woman), is a thing of which the smrti laws positively disapprove and as such make it a punishable offence. But they clearly distinguish between the offences involving the woman of the three categories stated above.

Another striking feature of the smrti law is the liability of the adulteress to be punished. Gautma states that the king should get an adulteress devoured by dogs in a public place, if the adulterer is of a caste lower than her.[33] The head of a brahmana adulteress is to be shaved, and her body to be anointed with butter; she is to be placed naked on a black donkey and to be taken round along the high road. According to Vasistha the woman becomes free thereby.[34] Manu departs from this rather lenient treatment. If a wife violates the duty which she owes to her lord, the king shall cause her to be devoured by dogs in a place frequented by many.[35]

---

31. Nar. XII. 70.
32. Nar. XII. 71.
33. Gaut. Dh. S. XXIII. 14.
34. Vas. Dh. S. XXI. 3.
35. Manu, VIII. 371.

REVENGE

The prescription of punishment is a clear recognition of the principle that such offences are no longer a private affair between individuals but a matter between the offender and the state, a matter with which the whole society is concerned. Inspite of this growth of social consciousness against individual crimes in the smrtis, we notice that the principle of revenge by the victims of the offender against the offender is given considerable and prominent place in the smrtis. Here we have the existence of the principle common to all ancient societies that evil should be returned for evil and that as a man deals with others he should himself be so dealt with. It is the dictum of an eye for an eye and a tooth for a tooth. We have already noted the provisions for cutting the 'tongue of a sudra for abusing virtuous person (Ap. Dh. S. II. 10.27.14), dropping of hot oil into his mouth for giving instructions to members of the highest caste (Visnu, V. 24) and the like. This is in consonance with the principle of revenge accepted during the Mauryan period according which that limb of the sudra with which he strikes brahmana must be cut off.[36] According to Visnu, with whatever limb an inferior insults or hurts his superior in caste the king shall deprive him of that limb.[37] For spitting both his lips and for abusive language his tongue shall be cut.[38] For striking out both eyes of a man the king should imprison him for life, or order him to be mutilated in the same way.[39] Manu lays down that with whatever limb a thief commits an offence the king should deprive him of that limb in order to prevent a repetition of that crime.[40] The principle of an eye for an eye and a tooth for a tooth lingers to the period of the later smrtis, and is evident from Narada's rule prescribing the cutting off of that limb of a man of low caste with which he

36. AS. BK. III. Ch. XIX.
37. Visnu, V. 19.
38. *Ibid.*, V. 21-23.
39. *Ibid.*, V. 71-72.
40. Manu, VIII. 334.

offends a brahmana.[41] Again with whatever organ of his body a thief acts, that very organ shall be taken from him.[42] Likewise Katyayana prescribes the cutting of the limb of a robber.[43]

The smrti law treats crimes not only as crimes as such but also as wrongs or Torts. Here the injure person recovers compensation in the shape of damages. A person who kills a ksatriya is to give a thousand cows the brahmanas for the expiation of his sin. Giving of a hundred cows for the death of a vaisya and ten for that of a sudra is prescribed.[44] Baudhayana prescribes similar compensation to the king for the killing of ksatriya, vaisya and sudra.[45] The provision to compel the slayer to make payment is similar to the laws of Germanic tribes where without an exception a system of money compensation for homicide as well as minor injuries was prescribed. But there appears to be a significant difference in the case of the smrti law according to which the compensation paid by the wrongdoers does not go to the party aggrieved but to the brahmana or the king. In this sense smrti laws consider the state or the society to be the party wronged, and the compensation bears the nature of expiation rather than providing of relief to the party aggrieved.

Manu rules in the smrti uphold the principle of wrath for wrath in dealing with the perpetrators of crime. Apastamba refers to a Purana which declares that slaying of an assailant does not involve sin for in that case wrath meets wrath.[46] Vasistha and Baudhayana state that a person who slays an assassin learned in the Veda and belonging to a noble family does not incur by that act the guilt of the murderer of a learned brahmana, because in that case "fury recoils upon fury."[47] Vasistha states that the slayer commits

---

41. Nar. XV-XVI. 25.
42. *Ibid.*, App. 34.
43. Kat. 822.
44. Ap. Dh. S., 1.24. 1-3.
45. Baud. Dh. S. 1.10.19. 1-3.
46. Ap. Dh. S. 1.10.29.7.
47. Vas. Dh. S.. III. 18; Baud. Dh. S. 1.10.18.13, Manu, VIII. 350-51.

no crime by killing an assassin.[48] He quotes approvingly the following verses:

"An incendiary, likewise, a poisoned, one who holds a weapon in his hand (ready to kill) a robber, he who takes away land, and he who abducts (another man's) wife, these six are called assassins (atatayin)."[49] Visnu describes assassins too be of seven kinds, those who try to kill with sword or with poison or with fire, those who raise their hands to pronounce a curse, those who raise a false accusation which reaches the ears of the king, and those having illicit connection with another man's wife.[50] Such persons who deprive others of their worldly fame or of their wealth or destroy religious merits by ruining pools or property such as houses and fields are also designated as assassin (atatayin). Brhaspati upholds the principle of revenge by stating that one commits no wrong by returning the abuse or giving blow for blow or striking the offender down.[51] Katyayana states clearly that an actual murderer is liable to be killed in various ways and goes further to state that one should certainly kill without waiting for consideration a man coming with the intention of destroying a life or a dam.[52]

No guilt is committed by killing a wicked man who is ready to kill another, but after, he desists from his attempt to kill he should be confined and not killed.[53] A significant departure introduced by Katyayana in the law relation to assassins is to limit the right of killing assassins only to cases where the assassins belong to any lower class. Referring to the views of Bhrgu he states that it is not proper to kill an atatayin who is superior in austerities, Vedic study and birth, killing is prescribed for sinner of a lower class.

A characteristic feature of the law of punishment in the smrtis is the extreme leniency with which brahmanas ae

48. Vas. Dh. S., III. 15.
49. *Ibid.*, III. 16.
50. Visnu, V. 191.
51. Br. XXI. 4.
52. Kat. 799.
53. *Ibid.*, 800.

treated in award of punishment. As a general principle Gautama no doubt states that if a learned man offends the punishment should be very much increased.[54] This principle however no where appears to be applied in the smrti laws while prescribing the punishment for different crimes excepting in cases of theft. Gautama himself contradicts the above principle when he states that corporal punishment must not be inflicted on a brahmana.[55] He ordains that the king must allow a brahmana immunity from six types of 'opprobrious treatment', i.e. he must not be subjected to corporal punishment. He must not be imprisoned, he must not be fined, he must not be exiled, and he must not be reviled nor be excluded.[56] Apastamba excludes the brahmanas from death penalty.[57] Santi Parva states that where a brahmana commits a crime, it is enough that he is ridiculed.[58] Visnu forbids infliction of corporal punishment on a brahmana but his lawgiver prescribes his banishment from his won county.[59] Narada firmly lays down that a brahmana on no account should be killed even if he is convicted of all possible crimes.[60]

Like Manu, who also forbids slaying a brahmana committing all possible crimes, he prescribes banishing of a brahmana offender.[61] Manu lays down the positive mandate that the king should leave all his property to the brahmana and his body should remain unhurt.[62] As a mandatory rule it is laid down that:

> "No grater crime is known on earth than slaying a brahmana; a king therefore, must not even conceive in his mind the thought of killing of brahmana."[63]

---

54. Gaut, Dh. S., VII.17
55. *Ibid.*, XII. 46.
56. *Ibid.*, VII. 12-13.
57. Ap. Dh. S., II. 5.11.1.
58. Sp. V. 2.3.
59. Visnu, V. 2.3.
60. Nar. V. 36.
61. *Ibid.*, App. 41: Manu, VIII. 380; Bar. XXVII. 11; Kat. 483.
62. Manu, VIII. 380.
63. *Ibid.*, VIII. 381.

Shaving the brahmana head, banishing him from the town, branding him on the forehead with a mark of the crime of which he is convicted, and parading him on an ass, are the punishments prescribed for such brahmanas.[64] Visnu prescribes that if the murderer belongs to the brahmana caste the figure of a headless corpse should be impressed on his forehead.[65]

Several other marks symbolizing the nature of crime are prescribed by the lawgivers.[66] Manu recommends a number of marks to be impressed on the forehead of the guilty brahmana such as the signs of tavern for drinking liquor, dog's foot for stealing headless corpse, and the mark of a female part for violation a Guru's bed.[67] There is, however, also faint discordant voice which does not exclude even a brahmana who is guilty of causing abortion, stealing gold, striking a brahmana woman with a sharp weapon or killing an innocent woman.[68]

CRIME, PUNISHMENT AND JUDICIAL PROCEDURE IN ANCIENT (SMRTI) INDIA

India's Culture is one of the oldest of the world. In ancient India danda was considered to be a crucial constituent of legal and social system. It was signified punishment meant for violating various laws of Society. These laws were framed and established by the ruling classes and on many points followed the principles of Varna or class legislation. The ultimate sanction behind the exercise of the State Authority lay in the power of the sword which depended on the power of king. Various Dharmashastras, material, demonstrate that judiciary was not only an important arm of Government, but also indispensable to the power structure known as the State. Let us consider first the

64. Nar. XIV. 10.
65. Visnu, V. 4.
66. *Ibid.*, V. 5-6.
67. Manu, IX. 238.
68. Yaj. II. 277; Kat. 806.

position of crime and punishment in smrti India or ancient India.

The smrtis prescribe various rules relating to. punishments to be awarded for different crimes. Abuse and defamation constituted an important crime, and may have originated frequently from prejudices based on castes, for the smrtis lay down punishments for offenders according to his caste. Narada's definition of Vakparusya also points to such a conclusion. He defines it as abusive speech couched in offensive and violent terms regarding the native, country, caste, family of a man, etc.[69] "The Gaudas are quarrelsome", "Brahmanas are extremely greedy", "persons of Visvamitra gotra commit cruel deeds", are a few examples of abuse of country, caste and family respectively.[70]

The nature of punishment as well as its degree prescribed in the smrtis appear to have the objective of preventing acrimony based on caste and the other prejudices and to maintain the social position of castes as laid down in vedas and smrtis. Gautama states that a sudra who intentionally reviles by criminal abuse or assault a member of the twice-born caste, is to be deprived of the limb with which he offends[71] and through punishments the sudras are sought to be excluded from learning the vedas. If he listens to recitations of the vedas intentionally, his ears are to be filled with molten tin or lac.[72] If he dares to recite the vedic texts his body is to be split.[73] For assuming equal position with members of the upper castes, corporal punishment is prescribed.[74] The anxiety of smrtis to preserve the varying social status of different castes is reflected also in the rules which prescribe different punishments for one and the same offence if they are committed by members of different castes. Thus if a Ksatriya abuses a Brahmana he is to pay a fine of

69. (Narda Smrti)—XV. 1.
70. P.V. Kane, (History of Dharma Sashtras), Vol. III, 511).
71. Gautam Dharma Sastra XII. I, Manu, VIII. 270, 279. 283.
72. Gautam Dharma Sastra XII. 4.
73. *Ibid.*, XII. 5.
74. *Ibid.*, XXI. 6.

hundred karsapanas, but in case a Brahmana abusing a Ksatriya only fifty, a vaisya only twenty five and nothing in the case of a sudra.[75] For a sudra Visnu prescribes a fine of twelve panas for abusing a man of one's own caste.[76] For abusing a member of lower castes the fine is only six panas.[77] If a Ksatriya defames a Brahmana he is to pay a fine of one hundred panas.[78] It When a Brahmana defames a Ksatriya he is to pay a fine of fifty panas, but in the case of defaming a vaisya and sudra a fine of only twenty five and twelve panas respectively.[79]

The fact that Manu makes abusing a sudra punishable with a fine of twelve panas whereas Gautama prescribes nothing. (Gautam Dh. S., XII. 13-14). It shows that during the time of Manu Sudra's position improved some what in this respect. Visnu also prescribes a fine of the first amercement for insulting a sudra.[80] At the same time Manu appears to be very stern and hard in dealing with the offences in which a twice-born man is insulted by a sudra; he prescribes cutting out of the tongue,[81] and thrusting into his mouth of red hot iron nail.[82] According to Manu if the sudra has the arrogance to teach brahmanas their duties the king should see that hot oil is poured into his mouth and into his ears.[83] The same is prescribed by visnu when a low born man mentions the name or caste of a superior revealingly.[84] The underlying principle behind the above discriminatory rule appears to) be that men of high social position must be protected against low persons and such low persons insulting a brahmana must be awarded severe punishment. Brhaspati states that persons begotten in the inverse order of caste and members of the

75. *Ibid.*, XII. 8-13; As B.K. III Ch. XVIII.
76. Visnu V-35.
77. Visnu V-36.
78. Manu, VIII, 267; Nar. XV-XVI. 15.
79. Manu VIII. 267; Nar. XV-XVI. 16; Br. XX. 7
80. Visnu, V. 103.
81. Manu. VIII. 270.
82. *Ibid.*, VIII. 271.
83. *Ibid.*, VIII. 272, Nar. XV-XVI. 24.
84. Visnu V-25, Nar. XV-XVI 23.

lowest caste are called the refuse of society; if they insult a brahmana they must be corporally punished and must never be amerced in a fine.[85] It is obvious that the nature and degree of punishment prescribed in the smrtis is discriminatory, and the discrimination itself is frankly justified. It has two dimensions. First, it is based on the caste of the person who commits the offence, secondly, it is based on the caste of the victim of such an offence. The combined objective of the whole provision is to preserve and enforce the system and caste inequalities with the help of the coercive power and machinery of the State.

The Arthasastra of Kautilya states that when a Ksatriya commits adultery on an unguarded brahmana woman a fine of the highest amercement is to be confiscated; in case of a Vaisya his entire property is to be confiscated; but a sudra is to be burnt alive.[86] Where a man commits adultery with a woman of low caste he is to be banished or degraded to the same caste. But in case of a sudra committing adultery with a woman of low caste he is to be put to death.[87] When a Sudra approaches a woman of Brahmana caste he is to be burnt alive.[88] When a Vaishya and Ksatriya approach a woman of the Brahmana caste they are to be burnt.[89] Similarly, when a Vaisya offends a Ksatriya woman, or when a sudra offends her or a Vaisya woman they are to be burnt.[90] In case involving adultery between a map of a twice-born caste with a woman of the sudra caste the man is to be banished.[91] But a sudra committing the same offence with a woman of first three castes, must suffer capital punishment.[92] In contrast to all these, where a Brahman commits adultery once with a married woman of equal class he needs only to

85. Brahaspath-(XXI.15).
86. Arthasastra-IV-Chapter XIII.
87. Arthasastra-IV-Chapter XIII.
88. Vasisth Dh. Sastra XXI I; (Gautam Dh. S. (XXIII.15).
89. *Ibid.*, XXI.23.
90. *Ibid.*, XXI. 4-5.
91. *Ibid.*, Dh. S. II. 10.27.8.
92. *Ibid.*, 11.10.27.9; Manu, VIII. 374.

perform one-fourth of the penance prescribed for an out caste.[93]

Punishment for offences relating to sex is not confined to only cases in which married woman are involved but; also covers criminal intercourse with women in general. If a man has criminal intercourse with an Aryan woman his organ is to be cut off, and all his property confiscated.[94] Apastmba prescribes for adultery the cutting of the organ of the adulterer but introduces a distinction in the crime of intercourse with a marriageable girl by providing the punishment of confiscation of property and banishment of the adulterer.[95] Manu recommends cutting of two fingers of the man forcibly contaminating a maiden besides making him pay six hundred panas as fine.[96] In the case of a man of equal caste defiling a willing maiden only a fine of two hundred panas is prescribed in order to deter him from a repetition of the offence.[97] If however, a sudra has intercourse with a woman of a twice-born caste punishment of loss of part and confiscation of property and even loss of life is provided.[98] According to Narada when a man has connections with a woman of his own caste a fine of the highest degree is prescribed, but when this involves a woman of lower caste the middling fine is prescribed. In case he has connections with a woman of superior caste capital punishment is to be awarded.[99] Narada also draws a distinction between connection of a man with a village woman; he prescribes severe punishment including death and confiscation of entire property in the later case if the woman belongs to the brahmna caste.[100]

---

93. Apastamba Dharma Sutra, S. II-10-27-11.
94. Gautam, Dh. S. XII.2.
95. Apastamba, Dh. S. II.10.26.20.
96. Manu, VIII.367.
97. *Ibid.*, VIII.368.
98. *Ibid.*, VIII.374.
99. Narda XII.70.
100. Narda XII.71.

Smrti laws seem to have appreciated clearly the difference in nature and gravity of sexual crimes involving woman belonging to another man (married woman adultery) and unwilling woman and a willing woman. Connections with a woman who is not one's wife (excepting certain categories of fallen woman), is a thing of which the smrti laws positively disapproved and as such make it a punishable offence. But they clearly distinguish between the offences involving the woman of three categories stated above.

Another striking feature of the smrti law is the liability of the adulteress to be punished. Gautama states that the King should get an adulteress devoured by dogs in a. public place, if the adulterer is of a caste lower than her.[101] The head of a brahmana adulterer is to be shaved, and her body to be anointed with butter; she is to be placed necked on a black donkey and to be taken round along the high road. According to Vasisth the woman becomes free thereby.[102] Manu departs from this rather, lenient treatment. If a wife violates the duty which she owes to her lord, the King shall cause her to be devoured by dogs in a place frequented by many.[103] The prescription of punishment is clear recognition of the principles that such offences are no longer a private affair between individual, but a matter between individual and state, a matter with which the whole society is concerned. Here we have the existence of the common principle to all ancient society that evil should be returned for evil. It is the dictum of an eye for an eye and a tooth for tooth, cutting the tongue of a sudra for abusing a Virtuous person and dropping of hot oil into his mouth for giving instruction to members of the high caste and like. According to Vishnu[104] with whatever limb an inferior insults or hurt his superior in caste the King shall deprive him that limb, for striking out both eyes of a man the king should imprison him for life or order him to be mutilated in the same way. Manu

101. Gautama Dh. S. XXIII-14.
102. Vasista Dh. S. XXI.3.
103. Manu, VIII. 371.
104. Vishnu Smrtis (V)-19, 21 to 23.

lays down that with whatever limb a thief commits an offence, the king should deprive him of that limb, in order to prevent a repetition of that crime.[105] It is also evident from Narada's rule[106] prescribing the cutting of that limb of a man of low caste with which he offends a brahmana. Likewise Katyayana[107] prescribes the cutting off the limb of a robber. The smrti law[108] treats crimes not only crimes as such but also as wrongs or torts. A person who kills a Ksatriya is to give 1000 cows to the Brahmans for the expiation of his sin, 100 cows for the murder of a Vaisya and 10 for the murder of Sudra. In this sense smrti laws consider the state or the society to be the party wronged and the compensation bears the nature rather than providing of relief to the party aggrieved:

Many rules in the ṣmrti uphold the principle of wrath for wrath in dealing with the Perpetrators of crime, Vasistha states[109] that the slayer commits no crime by killing an assassin. Baudhayna state that a person who slays an assassin learned in the vedas and belonging to a noble family does not incur by that act the guilt of the murderer of a learned Brahmana because in that case "fury recoils upon fury."[110] Now the question is who is assassin (Atatayin). Vasistha[111] prescribes six as follows: (A) who holds a weapon in his hand and read to kill, (B) robber, (C) he who take away land (D) he who abducts another man's wife, (E) an incendiary, (F) a poisoner. Vishnu described sever as follows: (i) Killing with sword, or (ii) with poison, or (iii) with fire, (iv) those who raised their hand to pronounce a curse, (v) False accusation which reaches to the ears of King, (vi) and those having illicit relation with another man's wife, (vii) lastly such persons who deprive other of their worldly fame or of

105. Manu-VIII-334.
106. Narda Purana XV.
107. Katyayana Smrti 822.
108. Bodhayana 1.10.19. 1-3.
109. Visatha Dah. S. III-15.
110. Baudhayana 1.10.18.13.
111. Visatha Dh. S. III-16.

their wealth or destroy religious merits by ruining pools or property such as houses and fields. Brhaspati[112] also upholds the principle of revenge by stating that one commits no wrong by returning the abuse or giving blow for blow or striking the offender down.

Katyayana[113] state clearly that an actual murderer is, liable to be killed in, various ways and goes further to state that one should certainly kill without waiting for consideration a man coming with the intention of destroying a life or dam. Katyayana also introduced a significant departure in the law relating to assassins to limit the right of killing assassins only to cases where the assassin belong to any lower class.

A characteristic feature of punishment in the smrti is the extreme leniency with which Brahamans are treated in award of punishment. Gautam[114] states that if a learned man offends, the punishment should be very much increased. This principle however no where appears to be applied in the smrti law while prescribing the punishment for different crimes except in case of theft. But he himself contradicts the principle when he states that corporal punishment must not be inflicted on a Brahmana. He further states that the King must allow a Brahmana immunity from six type of approbious treatment. He must not be imprisoned or punished otherwise in any manner. Apastamba[115] excludes the Brahmanas from death penalty. Vishnu[116] forbids infliction of corporal punishment a Brahmana but prescribes his expulsion from his own country. Likewise Narada[117] firmly lays down that a Brahmana should not be killed even if he is convicted of all possible crimes. Manu[118] laid down as follows: "No greater crime is known on earth than slaying Brahmana. A

112. Brhaspati Smrti XXI.4.
113. Katyayana Smrti 799.
114. Gautam Dharma Sastra VII 12.13 & 17, XII.
115. Apastamba Dharma Sastra II, 5, XI-(i).
116. Visnu Smrti V, 2, 3.
117. Narda Smrti V-36.
118. Manusmrti VIII-381, Manusmrti VIII-380.

king, therefore, must not even conceive in his mind it's thought." He had prescribed that the guilty Brahmana should be expelled and his entire property be left to Brahmanas. He had further prescribed[119] a number of marks to be impressed on the forehead of the guilty Brahmana such as the sign of tavern for drinking liquor, dog's foot for stealing headless corpse, and the mark of female part of violating a Guru's bed. Yajnavalkya smrti[120] also voices which does not exclude even a Brahmana who is guilty of causing abortion, stealing gold, striking a Brahmana woman with a sharp weapon or killing an innocent woman. Vishnu[121] prescribes that if the murderer belongs to the Brahmana caste the figure of headless corpse, should be impressed on his forehead.

Let us consider now the procedure for awarding punishment to culprits against their crimes.

Narada points out that the judicial proceeding has four feet, four bases and four means. It benefits four, reaches four and produces four results. Virtue, judicial proceedings, documentary evidence and royal edicts are the four feet of a law-suit, and each following gone one is superior to the one previously named. Here virtue is based on truth, judicial proceedings rest on statements of the witnesses, documentary evidence consists of declarations reduced to writing, and an edict depends on the pleasure of the King. Similarly, there are four parts of a trial. First, the connection (agama) must be examined, second, the title must be ascertained, third, the case and at end a decision is to be given. Because the four means of conciliation and the rest are adopted, it is said to have four means, and since judicial procedure protects the four orders it is said to benefit four. The four results of judicial proceedings are justice, gain, renown and esteem. Because the judicial procedure affects criminals witnesses, the assessors of the court, and the king to the amount of one quarter each, it is said to reach four. There are four parts of judicial proceedings such as declaration, answer, trial and deliberation of the judges. Regarding the *onus probandi*

119. Manusmrti, IX-238.
120. II.277.
121. Vishnu Smrti, V-4.

Narada emphasises that law suits are based on the statements of the two litigants. The accusation is called the plaint and the answer, the declaration of the defendant. The plaintiff should affirm his case first the defendant. When they have finished, the members of the Court (Sabhyas) and after them the judge should speak. The suitor stood before the Court bowing and the judge asked; "What is thy business? What is thy grievance? Fear not! speak out, O Man."

If the cause be judicially entertainable the judge should deliver the Court seal to the plaintiff for calling the defendant or he should order the court officer to call the defendant. The law suit could proceed further only when the court was convinced that a *prima facie* case was established by the plaintiff and it was entertainable judicially.

An officer of the court was to reduce to writing the statements of each party, and also whatever else has been written on the board, together with the names of the witnesses as well as the statements in which both parties concur. Accuracy in recording those statement is important, and the scribe who writes down the words of the plaintiff or the defendant differently from what they narrate is to be punished as a thief by the king who desires to enforce dharma. The additional statements of the plaintiff of defendant which are not contained in the writings of both parties are to be delinquently entered into their declaration. These are called pratyakalita, i.e. what is interposed.

If the plaintiff and defendant come into conflict claiming their own superiority or precedence, their declaration is to be received in the order of their castes, or after considering their grievances. Thus, the courts too were permeated in their practice and procedure with caste distinctions and privileges, which clearly shows the principles of procedure. This conclusion is strengthened by Narada's view there a sudra has no right to proffer a false accusation against a member of the twice-born caste, and if he does so his tongue shall be slit by the officers of the king and he shall be put on the stakes. In similar cases brahmanas are placed above every thing.[122]

122. Narada Smrti I, 8, 10, 11, 12, 13, 14, 15, 20, 21, 28, 36, 37, 40, 44.

Katyayan says: That if a litigant even when he has been asked to speak out, does not say anything, he deserves to be confined at once to the jail. He is also supposed to be losing party. It is presumed that he has to say nothing or the claim against him is valid in law. The principle that judgement should not be passed in the absence of parties seems to have been followed by the court. Katyayana further says even if defendant does not present himself when a decision is to be taken on usages, a gift of money, desirable actions and services, the King should not cause an error in decision by deciding in defendant's absence. The impartiality of the verdict is sought to be maintained by the rule that where a litigant induces even a single member of the Court to be partial towards him or where he offers a bribe, even to the opponent, he should be treated as a losing party to the dispute. In a civil dispute if a litigant himself threatens the other side or offers a bribe to him or gets him threatened or restrained through another person. He becomes Hinae' a losing party. It appears that the courts also acted as custodian of properties in dispute during the pendency of suit. Any property thus kept under the care of the judge must be returned to the winning party together with the interest accruing over it. Katyayana further lays down that if a litigant does not present himself before the Court after he is summoned, he loses his cause at once. Similarly, where a litigant desires to obtain more time or adjournment merely under a pretext he should be regarded as deceitful and such a conduct be declared to be a reason leading to the loss of the cause to him. There appears to be a realization that causes should be decided without delay and parties should not be permitted to absent themselves from providing information and thus cause delay in decision. Fresh trial of the cause is possible who has been defeated in accordance with texts speaking of hina (losing) litigant. There is however, no retrial for him who is defeated in accordance with texts that lay down expressly the loss of the matter in dispute. According to Narada,[123] however, a case could be tried once more, if a man was of the opinion that the suit has been

123. Yana Smrti, 199, 200, 201, 160, 204, 205, 208.

decided and punishment declared against him is in contravention to justice or texts, rules or judgment has not been given in a proper way provided he is prepared to pay twice the amounts of fine inflicted upon him. Narada[124] further describes legal proceedings of two kinds: (i) One, which is not attended by a wager, and (ii) secondly, when either of two parties stakes in writing a certain sum to be paid besides the amount in dispute; in case of defeat. Litigants are also supposed to provide sureties. If no surety provided by the plaintiff who has a proper cause for dispute, he is to be guarded and he has to give to the messenger guarding him, his wages at the end of the day. In the event of failure, three higher castes, he is to be guarded by wardens outside the lock up. But the sudras and others are to be confined and fettered if they cannot give sureties. It is, however, prescribed that persons of all castes should not be constructed in performing their obligatory rites and duties such as bathing, worshipping, Sandhya Prayer, etc. The Court would accept only competent surety. The master, an enemy, convict, under trial accused of certain categories, one appointed on the kings business or man of unsound mind could not be accepted as sureties. Strangers are not permitted to speak on behalf of others, if he is doing so, he is punished. Brother, father, son or authorised agent appear to have been permitted to speak on behalf of their litigant relations. But the victory or defeat would affect the party himself and not the representative. A representative is not allowed in cases involving murder of a brahmana, wine drinking, theft, indecent assault on another's wife, eating of forbidden food, kidnapping a maiden and intercourse with her, counterfeiting coins, measures, etc. In such cases the man himself should engage in the dispute.

Through Yajnavalkya Smrti[125] we come across various kinds of tribunals dispensing justice to the people such as assemblies of town dwellers, Companies of Traders and families. These are classified according to their relative importance in the investigation of the affairs of man and competent surety must be taken from both parties for the

---

124. Smrti 1, 4, 14, 22. 34, 65.
125. History of Dharma Sasthras.

satisfaction of the award. An appeal may be preferred from the decisions of family to person specially appointed by the ruler. The king shall reverse the cases decided by compulsion, by fear, by woman, at night inside a house, abroad and brought forward by enemies. Shree P.V. Kane[126] has summed up few other miscellaneous procedures from Dharmasastras as follows. Certain persons are exempted from personal appearance in the court and allowed to send their representatives. These include idiots, mad man, very old people, woman, boys or sick person for all of whom their kinsman or appointed agent are to give answers in the court. It appears that in a dispute of criminal nature no court fees are required to be paid. The person found guilty has to pay the king the fine declared in the smritis for offences. In civil disputes also nothing is paid as court-fees at the inception of the suit. Certain rules of course, do prescribe payments to the king but this has to be done after the decision of the suit. Such payments essentially partake the nature of Court fees.

The perusal of aforesaid provisions shows that the ancient smrtis and judicial system was complete in itself. This system, although discriminatory according to modern legal philosophy, but was maintaining the law and order of the then society. This system might be obsolete today, but it has distinctive characteristic features of its own. This system was having description of every kind of crime and punishment thereof the then present in ancient society. We may collect those distinguished noble principles which still best suits to the present society. These old and best suited principles may be adopted in the present legal system to boost the crippling judicial system. I am sure, if Indianization of the present legal system is adopted, then certainly legal system may be saved from collapse. We have to undertake a thorough research on this pattern to thrashout the grain from the chaff. We have to critically examine the old legal and judicial system for obtaining noble principles and giving up those principles which were either unwarranted to present day society or not meant for the welfare of society at all. Let us do needful in this direction.

---

126. Yajnavalkya Smrti, II-10, 18, 30, 31, 32.

Chapter

8

Ordeals

Provision for ordeal is a special feature of smrti litertrature. Almost all lawgivers belonging to the period 200 BC to 600 AD deal with ordeals.

The English term ordeal is of Titanic origin. It is a modified form of O.F. ordeal, the O.F. equivalent of a general Teutonic Term surviving in modern ordeal is a divine means to find out the truth in a dispute, which has been declared as outdated.[1] In Sanskrit the word divya is used to signify this system of test. Kane quotes definition of ordeals given in different authoritative books. In the Vyavahramayukha the term divya is defined as that which decides matter in dispute and which is not determined by human means of proof. The same meaning of divya is repeated elsewhere.[2] Therefore, divya denotes that system by which some supernatural force is prayed or invoked to intervene in a dispute in order to decide the guilt or innocence of the person involved. Jolly opines that the divine judgment is based on the belief in the direct intervention of the deity to vindicate the innocence or

1. Hasting's Encyclopaedia of Religion and Ehtics, Articles on ordeal, Introductory and Primitive, p. 7.
2. P.V. Kane, HDS, Vol. III, p. 363.

the expiate the violation of law which has occurred.[3] In the ordeal the party or witness where testimony is impeached calls upon Heaven to bear witness to his truth by saving his harmless from the fire.[4]

HISTORY OF ORDEALS

Trial of a case through ordeal is an 'ancient'[5] method, and it was practiced 'universally during a long period of social evolution'.[6] N.C. Sen Gupta says that 'divya' as a means of defense always existed from the earliest times.[7] In India the history of ordeals dates back to the Vedic period. Certain verses of the Rigveda indicate that fire and water ordeals were in vogue during the Vedic period (Rigveda, I. 158, 4, 5, III.53-22). Kane does not accept these as examples of ordeals.[8] Some western scholars hold that the Atharva Veda contains ideas regarding ordeals by fire and V.S. lends some support to this idea, but this is not universally accepted.[9] Pancavimsa or Tandya Brahmana (14.5.6.) refers to the story of Vatsa, who was accused by his step brother of being the son of a sudra woman. Vatsa protested against that and urged that he was a brahmana. He entered fore to prove the truth of his assertion and came out of it without any injury. Kane considers this as probably the earliest and the clearest reference in ancient Sanskrit literature to the ordeal of fire.[10] The Kausika Sutra (III.8) seems to refer to the ordeal by the hot piece of gold. In a passage of the Satapatha Brahmana (XI.2.733) a reference to the balance ordeals as practiced in later Vedic times is found.

---

3. Jolly, Hindu Law and Custom, p. 310.
4. Fitzgerald, P.J., Salmond on Jurisprudence, pp. 473-74.
5. Spellman, Political Thought of Ancient India, p. 119.
6. H.L. Lee, Superstition and Force, p. 218.
7. N.C. Sen Gupta, Evolution of Ancient Indian Law, p. 61.
8. P.V. Kane, HDS, Vol. III, p. 361.
9. Spellman, Political Thought in Ancient India.
10. P.V. Kane, HDS, Vol. III, p. 362.

In Dharmasutras we get the only reference to ordeal in Apastamba (II.11.29.6.), when he considers ordeals as a way of deciding disputed. Kautilya too totally ignores these ordeals. Among the writers of metrical smrtis Manu was the first to assert the idea that ordeals constituted a definite part of the judicial procedure prevailing during that period. But Manu did not develop the system of ordeals in a systematic manner. Yajnavalkya and Visnu were the first to develop the system of ordeals.[11] After that the other lawgivers developed the system in a more comprehensive way. In non-juristic literature too we find stray references to ordeals. The Mahabharata (III.134.27) mentions a man proving an accusation by entering the water, and a fire ordeal seems to have been referred to in Sita's vindication of herself in the Ramayana (VI.16) (A.B. Keith opinions that these events give a very vague sense of ordeals as found in Manu).[12]

Certain dramas such as the Mrachakatika (Act IX, 43), Kadambari, etc. contain the idea that ordeals were practiced in the early century of the Christian era.[13] Certain digests and commentaries such as the Mitaksara, the Smrticandrika, the Divyatattva of Raghunandana, and the Vyavahara Mayukha also describe these ordeals elaborately.[14]

TYPES OF ORDEALS

Here we propose of discuss ordeals which are described in the metiacal smrtis. Ordeal by fire and water are the oldest types. The msrti-writes do not agree on the number and types of ordeals to be practiced in various cases. Manu was the first among such writers to describe ordeals already known and practiced. He mentions only two types of ordeals, ordeal by fore and ordeal by water.[15]

---

11. Hasting's Encyclopaedia of Religion and Ethics, p. 522.
12. *Ibid.*, p. 524.
13. Quoted by Kane. HDS, Vol. III, p. 362.
14. *Ibid.*
15. Manu, VIII. 114.

Yajanvalkya, who ranks second among the smrti-writers, enumerates five types of ordeals, such as by balance, water, fire, poison and sacred libation.[16] Visnu and Narada also agree with Yajnavalkya so far the number and types of ordeals were concerned.[17] Katyayana mentions seven types, whereas Brhaspati's list includes nine types of ordeals. They are ordeals by balance, fire, water, poison, sacred libation, grains of rice, a hot piece of gold, ploughshare and ordeal by Dharma.[18]

What were the circumstances under which ordeals were prescribed? In normal cases ordeals were not recommended. The smrti-writers suggest various types of situations. Manu says that if no witness is available in any dispute and the judge is unable to ascertain the truth oath could be taken.[19] probably he considers such a situation as suitable for the use of trial by ordeal. Yajnavalkya suggests the use of ordeal in the case where the king is a party and the accusation is serious.[20] Katyayana describes several types of circumstances under which ordeals could be practiced.[21] First, he says that in the case of the failure of agreement one should take recourse to ordeal.[22] Thirdly, where the witnesses are equal the judge should fond out the truth by means of ordeals.[23] Lastly, he opines that in all those cases, which entail death penalty, ordeals could be practiced.[24] Brhaspati too agrees with the other writers and suggests that even though there be witness for deciding a criminal case of serious nature and appropriation of a deposit, the king should take the help of ordeals.[25] He further says that forger of hems, pearls or

16. Yaj. II.95.
17. Visnu, IX. 10-1: Nar. I 252.
18. Br. X 4-05.
19. Manu, VIII. 109.
20. Yaj. II. 96.
21. Kat. II. 96.
21. Kat. 237.
22. *Ibid.*, 238.
23. *Ibid.*, 232.
24. *Ibid.*, 232.
25. Br. X 2.

corals, one withholding a deposit, ruffian, and adulterer could be tried by ordeal even though there he witnesses.[26] Brhaspati also prescribes that when a thing has happened long ago or in secret, or when the witnesses have disappeared long or are perjured, ordeals should be adopted.[27] In case of doubt with regard to a document oral evidence, or in the case of the failure of argument ordeals should be practiced.[28] Visnu prescribes the use of ordeals indiscriminately when a criminal case is directed against the king, or in the cases of violence.[29] Further in the case of a deal of deposit or in the case of theft or robbery ordeals should be adopted.[30] Narada also advises the use of ordeals in the absence of witnesses,[31] or in the case of heavy crime[32] or in certain doubtful case, which has become the object of lawsuit, especially of the matter under dispute is of a recondite nature.[33]

SCOPE OF ORDEALS

The ordeals extended over a wide field of jurisdiction. Civil as well as criminal cases covered by them. In serious cases their use was considered compulsory as even the presence of witness in such cases was ignored. It could be used also in the case of treason. The review of verses concerning ordeals give us some idea regarding their salient features. Divinity is a distinctive feature of ordeals. It is unanimously accepted by the smrti writers that ordeals are ordained by some divine power. Secondly, arbitrary execution ordeals were not prescribed. Arbitrary use is prohibited by Brhaspati who ordains that ordeals to be administered, should correspond to the amount of the administered, should correspond to the amount of the sum in dispute and to the

26. *Ibid.*, X1.
27. Br. X3.
28. *Ibid.*, X.17.
29. Visnu, IX.22.
30. *Ibid.*, IX.3.
31. Nar. I. 247.
32. *Ibid.*, I. 249.
33. *Ibid.*, I. 251.

character or strength of the individual.[34] Katyayana also repeats the same idea.[35] Visnu also holds that ordeals should be administerd according to the value of the property claimed.[36] Narada prohibits the arbitrary use of ordeal by saying that ordeals must be appropriate to the place, to the season and to the strength of the defendant.[37] So the authorities could not prescribe ordeals in an arbitrary manner, but they had to take into consideration many factors such as the time of occurrence of the crime, the physical capacity of the defendant, the mount involved in the dispute, etc.

Another marked characteristic of ordeals is that different ordeals have been prescribed for different disputes. Manu does not say anything clear about it. Yajnavalkya is a bit more specific. He states that ordeals by balance ,water, fire, poison and sacred libation are meant for deciding grave disputes.[38] Brhaspati and Narada enumerate separately various cases. For civil cases certain ordeals are prescribed. According to Brhaspati the ordeal by poison should be administered when property worth a thousand panas is stolen.[39] Ordeals by fire was prescribed when a quarter less than the above mentioned amount has been stolen[40] If there is a charge for the theft of four hundred panas the hot piece of gold should be administered. In case it is worth three hundred, the grains of rice should be given. The ordeal by sacred libation was provided when the case was concerned with half the amount.[41] When a hundred pana is stolen or falsely denied purgation by Dharma should be administered. Thieves of cow should be subjected by preference to the ordeal by the ploughshare by the judges.[42] Narada declares

34. Br. X8.
35. Kat. 237.
36. Visnu, IX.22.
37. Nar. I. 239.
38. Yaj. II. 95.
39. Br. X. 9.
40. *Ibid.*, X. 9.
41. *Ibid.*, X 10.
42. *Ibid.*, X. 11.

that five types of ordeals shall be administered in cases of heavy charges.[43] Rice ordeals should be administration only in the case of larceny and in other cases.[44] The ordeal by a hot piece of gold should be used for distinguishing virtue or vice.[45]

Varna distinction is another characteristic of the system of ordeal. Manu does not pay any attention towards this. But Yajavalkya mentions caste distinction when he reserves the ordeal by balance for brahmana only.[46] Narada agrees with Yajanavalkya on this point.[47] Katyayana suggests that the king should prescribe the ordeal of fire for a ksatriya, balance for a brahmana and water for a vaisya, or he may fix any ordeal for all castes but the ordeal of poison should never be administered in the case of a brahmana.[48]

Another distinguishing feature of the system of ordeal is that not only caste distinction was taken into consideration while prescribing ordeals but also the physical capacity of the person. On this point too Manu is silent while other writers on smrtis pay attention towards this. Narada reserved ordeal by balance for eunuchs, distressed or feeble persons, the severely afflicted, infants, old men and women and the blind.[49] Having taken into consideration the physical capacity of persons Yajnavalkya suggests ordeal by balance for women, minors, old men, the blind, lame and sick persons.[50] For strongmen ordeal by fire, water or poison is prescribed; it is also laid down for persons who gain their subsistence from water such as fishermen and the like.[51]

The timing for the administration of ordeals was also prescribed. Manu Katyayana and Brhaspati do not prescribe any particular reason for administering any particular ordeal.

43. Nar. I. 336.
44. *Ibid.*, I. 37.
45. *Ibid.*, I. 334.
46. Nar. II. 98.
47. Nar. I. 334-35.
48. Kat. 422.
49. Nar. VI.8.
50. Yaj. II. 98.
51. Visnu, IX. 25.29.

Narada prescribes ordeal by fire during the rainy season,[52] by water during the summer season,[53] and during the winter seasons the ordeal by poison was to be administered. At the same time Narada states that ordeal by balance should be practiced in the autumn season.[54] Visnu too prescribes various seasons for various ordeals.[55]

The system of ordeals was voluntary in nature. Excepting a few cases it was generally administered according to the onsent of both the parties. Narada suggests that the king or the chief judge should not administer anyone of the fire ordeals without the consent of both the parties.[56]

Another distinctive feature of the system of ordeal was its irrationality: it was based upon superstitious belief. Brhaspati describing the process of sacred libation says that if no calamity happens within a week or a fortnight either to the accused or to his son, wife or property, he has to be considered innocent.[57] Several examples prove that these ordeals had no logical basis. Such evils might befall even innocent people. Therefore, we find that the element of chance is also involved in the system of ordeals.

Certain exemptions were also allowed. Narada rules out ordeal by water in the case of the distressed person, by poison in the case of the bilious, by fire in the case of afflicted with white leprosy, or with blindness or with bad nails.[58] According to him an ordeal should never be administered to persons engaged in performing a vow, to those affected with a heavy calamity, to the diseased, to those afflicted with a heavy calamity, to the diseased, to ascetics or to women.[59] Katyayana prohibits the administration of ordeal profession-wise. He state that ordeal by fire shall not apply to

---

52. Nar. I. 254.
53. *Ibid.*, I. 254.
54. *Ibid.*, I. 254.
55. Visnu, X 26.28.30.
56. Nar. I. 258.
57. Br. X 24; Visnu, XV. 4.
58. Nar. I. 255.
59. Nar. I. 256.

blacksmiths, by water to those who ply watercraft, and by poison to those who are experts in mantras and yoga practice; he should not appoint tandulas to his who is observing a vow.[60] Exemptions were allowed also in the case of certain disease. Ordeal by fire was not applicable to lepers, and by water to those persons who suffer form breathing difficulty and cough. Poison ordeal was not advised in the case of persons suffering form excess of bile.[61]

Ordeals were executed in public. Secrecy regarding its proceedings was not maintained. It is stated that ordeal by balance should be administered in the midst of a public assembly or within the sight of a temple or on a crossroad.[62] It is laid down that ordeal by balance should never be administered at a solitary place but publicly in the presence of the guardians of the world who must be invoked to be present for the protection of virtue and justice.[63] Narada says that ordeal by water may be administered in the streams which do not flow too swiftly, in oceans, in rivers, in lakes, in ponds dug by the gods, in tanks, etc.[64] Although Katyayana prefers the public places for different cases. According to him the king should employ ordeals in a well, or in a known temple, in the case of men who are accused of grave sin and near the royal gate in the case of those who engage in treason. Ordeal should be offered in a public square where four roads meet to those who were the progeny of the mixed castes.[65] Manu does not say anything about the place of execution of ordeals, but administered in the presence of a brahmana.[66] Visnu adds that ordeals should be administered in the presence of the images of god and of assessor. Certain religious performances preceded the execution of ordeal. Prayers were offered to gods and to natural phenomena to prove the truth.

---

60. Kat. 424.
61. *Ibid.*, 425.
62. Nar. I. 265.
63. *Ibid.*, I 267.
64. *Ibid.*, I. 305.
65. Kat. 434.
66. Visnu, X. 33; Yaj. 71.97.

What were the aims of the ordeals? Narada analyzing the aim of ordeal, point out that the ordeals are ordained for the purpose of proving the innocence of the criminals who are defendant in lawsuits.[67] Katyayana agrees that ordeals were meant for finding out truth.[68] Ordeals were practiced to serve some other purposes such as the eradication of unsocial elements from society so that moral standards of a higher level could be maintained. Brhaspati says that some persons must be tested by ordeals even of witnesses are available. They are the forger of hems, pearl, coral, one withholding a deposit, ruffian and an adulterer, etc.[69] Apart from these conclusion regarding the aims and objectives of these ordeals one can think of another aim also. The metrical smrtis were mainly brahmanical works, and they were written with the purpose of the preservation of the brahmanical social order.

SANCTION BEHIND ORDEALS

The review of several verses concerned with ordeal testifies that these ordeals lacked any legal sanction though in a verse of Narada we also come across an idea that if the defendant is acquitted he should be given hundred and fifth panas as fine.[70] Visnu also advocated the above system.[71] Only religious sanction could be assigned to these ordeals. It is stated by the majority of the smrti writers that something might befall upon the evildoer. This fear compelled them to accept the verdict, which emerged when these ordeals were practiced.

PERSONNEL ENGAGED IN ORDEAL

In Gupta times the king was the repository of all powers including the judicial power. Hence he was also the

67. Nar. I. 253.
68. Kat. 232.
69. Br. X. 1.
70. Nar. I. 336.
71. Visnu, IX. 20.

ultimate authority to execute these ordeals. Manu does not state specifically that the king was responsible for the execution of ordeals. He entrusts this duty only to the judges.[72] Yajnavalkya makes both king and brahmansa responsible for enforcing the ordeals.[73] Katyayana favours the appointment of certain experts when he states that those who are adept in the knowledge of ordeals should offer ordeals to the defendant.[74] Brhaspati also emphasizes the importance of experts in the administration of ordeals. He says that ordeals should be administered by persons acquainted with the rules of ordeals otherwise they will prove to be ineffective.[75] In addition to these experts Brhaspati also favours the idea of the appointment of certain examiners. Narada also agrees with Brahaspati on this point when he states that certain examiners are always required to take care that the scales of the balance should be equal.[76] Narada further provides for the appointment of certain experienced persons to ascertain the weight of the man and the arch marked at the height, which corresponded to the even position of the two scales.[77]

It is quite evident that some lower staff was needed for this purpose. Narada and Visnu mention those persons who should be appointed in the case of different ordeal to discharge certain menial duties. Both suggest the appointment of goldsmith and braziers in the case of ordeal by balance.[78] Narada further suggests the appointment of certain other persons at the time of the administration of the ordeal by balance. They are merchants.[79] In the case of ordeal by fire a professional blacksmith, who has skill in working with fire, and whose skill has been tested on previous occasions, should be caused to heat the iron in fire.[80] Persons well versed in

72. Manu, VIII. 14.
73. Yaj. II. V. XCVII.
74. Nar. 244.
75. Br. X. 18.
76. Nar. I. 274.
77. *Ibid.*, I. 273.
78. *Ibid.*, I. 274; Visnu, XV. 4.
79. Nar. I.274.
80. *Ibid.*, I. 288.

law should fox the exact quantity of the poison to be given[81] Hence we find that the execution of ordeal required the services of a large number of people other than the king and judge. The law givers devoted much time to the discussion of the ordeal. That these ordeals were really enforced, is testified by Yuan Chwang who while traveling in India noted that four kings of ordeals were in vogue. He states, "These are by water, by fire weighing and by poison."[82] Till recently we get stray references to these practices in India. We may also conclude that these ordeals were precised in order to several double purpose, i.e. to scare the people and also to establish the supremacy of the brahmana class.

In the modern state ordeal have no place at all. Among the three superstitious methods ordeals, trial by battle and oath, which commended themselves so strongly to the wisdom of the ancients, only the last one, i.e. oath persists even today as a remnant of man's reliance on appeal to the super natural in his quest for truth and justice.

81. *Ibid.*, I. 319.

82. Quoted by H.N. Sinha, Sovereignty in Ancient Indian Polity, p. 281.

Chapter

9

Property Law

Strengthening of private property appears to be one of the objects of the smrti law. Private property in both the movables and immovable, had been in existence from earlier times. The institution of Gana in which men did not distinguish between 'mine' and 'thine' was a thing to the past; the Santi Parva contains references revealing the mind and attitude of man towards wealth. Everybody has the ambition to possess wealth as his own property.[1] Some of the ideas regarding property remind us of the gana days, and wealth and private property are considered to be the causes of conflict and jealousies in society. The pursuit of wealth makes it very difficult for men to give up acts, which should not be done there. There appears a conflict between wealth and dharma.[2] Yudhisthira states that it is difficult to find goodness among those who are after wealth for they alone get wealth ho come in conflict with others.[3] Arjun, on the other hand, emphasizes the brighter aspects of wealth in society. Loss of wealth leads less of dharma. People consider

1. SP, 130.46.
2. *Ibid.*, 26.18-19.
3. *Ibid.*, 26.20.

a poor man to be like one fallen from dharma. There is no difference between these two.[4] Wealth assumes such an importance that through it dharam, kama and sverga are fulfilled.[5] Wealth leads to abundance of friends and between bandhavas only those having wealth are considered to be scholars (pandita) and deserve admiration.[6]

Property is weakness; wealth makes one strong. A wealthy person has everything available for himself.[7] Wealth enables even a sudra to subjugate persons who are superior to him, and as such he must not collect wealth.[8]

In the Santi Parva wealth is, however, fettered with great limitations with regard to its applications. It is said to have been created by God for the purpose of Yajan, and as such the entire wealth should be used for it. Its use for pleasure (bhoga) is neither beneficial not good.[9] It is not proper for the king to have his eyes on the wealth of the brahmana even in times of extreme urgency. Donation of wealth to the brahmanas leads one to heaven.[10] A king shall be considered very inferior if he does not make gift of horses, cows, female slaves (dasi), elephants, village, field, house, etc. to the brahmanas.[11] It is not enough that the king should make donations of wealth and property to a brahmana; he must not also lay his hands on the property of the brahmanas and gods.[12] The wealth or property of the brahmanas should be safeguarded by the king in the same way as he should be safeguarded by the king in the same way as he should safeguard the brahmanas.[13] If the wealth of the brahmanas is safeguarded everything is saved.[14] In this way the brahmanas

4. SP, 8.13-15.
5. *Ibid.*, 8.17; 130.15.
6. SP, 8.19.
7. *Ibid.*, 130.49.
8. *Ibid.*, 60.30.
9. *Ibid.*, 26.25.
10. *Ibid.*, 22.23.
11. *Ibid.*, 12.30-31.
12. *Ibid.*, 136.2.
13. *Ibid.*, 75.11.
14. *Ibid.*, 75.12.

emerge as a class owning wealth and property, and it is the duty of the king to safeguard this wealth. It appears that the rules lay down by the smrti-kars aim at creating a powerful brahmana class of property owners. Gautama states that the reward of gift, offered to a non-brahmana is two-fold; to a srotriya thousand fold and to one who knows the whole Veda endless.[15] A gift of land and money to the brahmanas enables the king to gain endless worlds.[16] A king who feels his end drawing near shall bestow all his wealth, accumulated from fines, on the brahmanas.[17] Narada lays down that when a person gives any property to a brahmana the king must give his consent to it.[18] Brhaspati asks the king to grant the brahmans landed property and house.[19]

Hence it is clear that smrtis and the Santi Parva applaud the virtues of making to the brahmanas gifts of properties. This is, however not the chief contribution of the smrtis, for grant of lands to the brahmanas was already prevalent.[20] Even Kautilya lays down that those who perform sacrifices, spiritual guilds, priests, and those learned in the Vedas should be granted brahmanya lands yielding sufficient produce and exempted from taxes and fines.[21] The main characteristic of the smrti rules in this regard appears to be the strengthening of the property rights of the brahmanas against everybody else, including the king. The treasure trove of the brahmanas is given immunity, whereas those of all others belong to the king.[22] The king should not take for himself the property of brahmana, for the overawing reason that "the property of brahmana destroys (him who takes it), together with sons and grandsons, poison kills one man only.

15. Gaut. Dh. S. V.19.
16. Ap. Dh. S. II. 10.26.1.
17. Manu, IX. 323.
18. Visnu, III.81.
19. Nar. XVIII. 47.
20. Br. XVII.3.
21. AS, BK. II. Ch. I.
22. Gaut. DH. S. Ch. I.

(Therefore) they do not declare poison to be (the worst) poison."[23]

The property of a brahmana is, therefore, a terrible poison for him who takes it.[24] While the king may take the property of men of other castes, on failure of all heirs, he is forbidden to do so with respect to the property of the brahmanas.[25] The sinful man. Who through covetousness, seizes the property of the gods, or the property of the brahmanas feeds in another world on the leavings of the vultures.[26] A person shall be banished of the embezzles the goods belonging to a corporation of brahmanas or the goods which have been lent to them by the king or by private persons.[27] Properties bestowed on persons other than a brahmana may be resumed, but not those of the brahmanas.[28]

Later smrtis do not appear to be satisfied merely with recommending gifts to the brahmanas but desire that full proof of titles to property be given to them. According to Visnu a document of proof must be given to the man upon whom land is bestowed. This document not only serves as a proof against the ruler bestowing the gift, but also seeks to perpetuate the title of the dinee against all future kings. It is enjoined that the document should mention the area of the land bestowed and contain an impreciation against "him who should appropriate the donation himself."[29] Brhaspati prescribes the giving of a document in which the remissions of revenue are specified.[30] The gift should last as long as the moon and sun last and descend by right of inheritance to the son, grandson, and more remote descendant. The gift should be such as may not be cut down or taken away and should

23. Baud, Dh. S., 1.5.11.16; Vas. Dh. S. XVII. 86.
24. Vas. Dh. S. XVII. 85.
25. Manu, IV. 189; Visnu, III. 83.; Br. XXI. 67-68.
26. Manu, XI. 26.
27. Visnu, V. 167.
28. Nar. XVIII. 49.
29. Visnu, III. 82.
30. Br. XVII. 3.

be e entirely exempt from diminution.[31] It is thus evident that the laws enunciated in the smrtis not only strengthen the rights of the Brahmanas to receive and hold their private properties but also impart to such properties the character of permanency with a new sanctity attached to the gifted property. Its undisturbed enjoyment is now assured against everybody including the king himself.

Along with the strengthening of the position of the brahmanas with regard to their landed property and other possession, the smrti laws also contributed to the strengthening of the institution of private property in general. Even though private property as an economic institution had emerged in the society before the beginning of the Christian era it suffered from many limitations, the most important of these being royal restrictions, and interference and the violation of private property by the king himself. It is theoretically conceded in Santi Parva that according Vedic principles the king enjoys right over the properties of all excepting those belonging to brahmanas.[32] The king has the right to take away the wealth or property of everybody excepting that of the brahmanas.[33] During the times of emergency he is advised not to suffer on account of the paucity of wealth and is granted the liberty of taking by force the wealth of the rich. It is significant to note that the above authorization of encroachment on property is made along with the recognition that if the king does not protect it will not be possible to have wealth and household and all property will vanish.[34] It is admitted that in the absence of protection from the king persons owning wealth will be the object of restrictions and slaying and they would not be in a position to claim anything as their own.[35]

In contrast with the above views expressed in the Santi Parva the smrti laws emphasize the sanctity of private

31. *Ibid.*, VIII. 17.
32. SP, 26.10.
33. *Ibid.*, 130.20.
34. *Ibid.*, 68.15.
35. *Ibid.*, 68.19.

property and clear rules are laid down t: this effect. The king is advised not to take property for his own use form the inhabitants of his realm.[36] Yajnavalkya lays down that the king shall not collect fines unjustly, and if he does so he is required to return to the pèrson the amount so taken.[37] Brhaspati states that when land is taken from one man by a king actuated by anger, avarice, or by using a fraudulent pretest, and bestowed on a different person as a mark of his favour, such a gifts is not valid.[38] Yajnavalkya ordains the king not to interfere with the attempt on the part of a creditor to recover his wealth or money, and in the event of a complaint being lodged before him the king should get the payment made by the debtor and also punish such a defaulting debtor.[39] Acquiring wealth by war and giving of property to the brahmanas are deemed to be the highest virtues of kings, but at the same time giving constant security to his subjects, is also considered a virtue. Visnu states that one who has taken by force any property belonging to another inevitably enters other than gold becomes a felon. In a society dominated very much by religion and belief in transmigration of soul such rules are perhaps laid down with the objective of inculcating among men a respect for property belonging to others and deterring a potential thief from violating it through such fears.[40] Apastamba declares that a person devouring and taking other man's possessions under any condition whatsoever is a thief.[41] Narada states that a man who forcibly enjoys property such as a house, field, cow or the like, without authorization from the owner, deserves the same punishment as a thief. Kautilya prescribes beheading of person who wantonly murders or steals a herd of cattle.[42]

In the initial stages when law and order had not

36. Vas. Dh. S., XIV. 14.
37. Yaj. II. 307.
38. Br. XIX. 22.
39. Yaj. II. 40.
40. Visnu, XLIV. 44.
41. Ap. Dh. S. 1.10.28.1.
42. AS. BK. IV. Ch. X.

stabilized, encroachments on the property of weaker sections was more likely. Perhaps with this in view Gautama makes it a responsibility of the king to protect the property of the infant or minors till they attain their majority or complete their studentship.[43] The king should guard the property of men belonging to a non-brahmanical caste, the owner of which has not appeared for a year.[44] Vasistha lays that the king should protect what has been gained, the property of the infants of royal family and of persons unfit to transact legal business such as minors, widows, etc.[45] The Arthasastra of Kautilya lays down that the king shall protect agriculture form the molestation of oppressive fines, poisonous creatures and cattle diseases.[46] A householder's house and his field are considered as two 'fundaments' of his existence, and therefore the king is ordained not to upset either of them.[47] Echoing the Arthasastra, Narada makes the interests of the king and those of the people harmonious. The religious merits of the king and increase in his treasure depend on the flourishing of his people.[48] The society being essentially agricultural, householder can thrive only if his properties, i.e. his house and his field, are not encroached as and institution complementary to the interests of the king and his treasurer rather than contradictory to these.

As land became a valuable property the question of violation of its boundaries came to therefore. In order that owners of land may cultivate the fields peacefully, violation of boundaries, encroachments on others. Land, and taking of land by threats, are considered to be crime of the first, second and third amercement respectively.[49] The Arthasastra of Kautilya provides detailed arrangements for investigation and settlement of boundary disputes between two villages.[50]

---

43. Gaut, Dh. S. X. 48; Manu, VIII. 27.
44. Baud. Dh. S. 1.10.18.16.
45. Vas. Dh. S. XVI. 6-9.
46. AS. BK. II. Ch. I.
47. Nar. XI. 42.
48. Nar. XI. 43; AS. BK. I, Ch. XIX.
49. Yaj. II. 155.
50. AS. BK. III. Ch. IX.

Punishment is provided for encroachments upon and destruction of boundaries. Narada thinks that boundary should not be fixed by a single person even if he is reliable; he entrusts this business to several persons because "it is an affair of importance.[51] "The importance of landed property and its boundaries is so great that in the absences of proper persons conversant with the true state of the question the king is advised to fix the boundary between the lands himself.[52] It is an essential attribute of property that the owner should use, consume, or enjoy it without let, or hindrances or any other injury. The smrtis contain rules which when peacefully employed facilitate enjoyment of the property and appropriation of its usufructs, under the protective unbrella of the state. The Arthasastra of Kautilya lays down that those who drive cattle through field without intimation to the owner shall be fined if crops are eaten away by the animals. The owners of the cattle shall, of proved guilty, pay twice the amount of loss.[53] Visnu provides for compensation to the owner of the field to the extent of the value of the grain destroyed.[54] Different scales of punishment are provided for damages caused by different animals depending upon their capacity to cause damage.[55] If a cultivator or a neighbour makes an encroachment upon a field• during the time of sowing seeds he is to be fined.[56] A person obstructing or causing any king of mischief to the flow of water is to be punished.[57] If damage is caused while making use of tanks, rivers etc., to the sees sown in the fields of others the person responsible is to pay compensation equivalent to the damage.[58] In order to encourage the use of irrigation of better production provision has been made by

51. *Ibid.*, p. 169.
52. Nar. XI. 9-11.
53. AS. BK. III. Ch. X.
54. Visnu, V. 146; Nar. XI. 29.
55. Yaj. II. 159; Kat. 667; Manu, VIII. 241.
56. AS. BK. III. Ch. X.
57. *Ibid.*, p. 172.
58. *Ibid.* p. 169.

Kautilya for remission of taxes for five years of new works such as tanks, lakes, etc. are constructed, and for four years of repair is done to neglected or ruined works of similar nature.[59] The Arthasastra lays down that the king should construct reservoirs (setu) filled with either perennial or drawn from other sounces.[60] pasture lands, plans and forests may be used by the owners for grazing their cattle.[61] The unhindered cultivation of land by the husbandman is given so much impotence that Katyayana even forbids the arrest of the husbandman during the sowing season. When the husbandman is about to reap the prop or when the rainy season approaches the plaintiff should not make such a defendant engaged in dispute from the beginning of the sowing of seeds to the gathering in of the corps. If the plaintiff arrests one who should both arrested he should be punished according Katyayana.[62]

According to the smrtis it is the responsibility of the king to give compensation to a subject whose property is stolen and not recovered.[63] Earlier Gautama states that the king having recovered property stolen by a thief should return it to the owner. In the event of his failure to recover the property the king should pay its value to the owner out of his treasury.[64] It is significant to mote that while Apastamba makes the government servants responsible for protection of towns and villages and liable to pay compensation of property stolen but not recovered, the later smrtis make the king himself responsible for the payment of such compensation.[65] Severe punishments is prescribed for theft which appears to be one of the rare crimes, in which the quantum of punishment prescribed runs contrary to the general trend of giving lighter punishment to the higher

---

59. *Ibid.,* p. 170.
60. AS. BK. II. Ch. I.
61. *Ibid.,* BK. III. CH. X.
62. Kat. 109-110; Br. II. 37.
63. Manu, VIII. 40.
64. Gaut. DH. S. X. 46-47; Yaj. II. 36; Visnu, III. 66-67; Kat. 813-17.
65. AP. Dh. S. II. 10.26.8.

castes. According to Gautama a sudra acquiring property unrighteously by theft must be made to repay eight-fold the value involved, but for each of the other castes fines must be doubled till it reaches the maximum of sixty four-fold in the case of a learned man.[66] Narada details the scale of fine for a sudra as eight-fold, for a vaisya sixteen-fold, for a Kastriya thirty-fold, and for a brahmanas sixtyfour-fold.[67] The great importance and scarcity attached to property in the smrtis is also evident from the statement of Gautama. According to him if a witness vives false evidence regarding small cattle he kills ten but as regards cows, houses, men or land, he kills in each succeeding case ten times as many as in the one mentioned before. He adds that through false evidence regarding land he kills the whole human race and that hell is the punishment for theft of land.[68] Haradatta interprets that the offender incurs the same guilt as he does in actually killing human beings, and the punishment is the same.[69] The qauantum of punishment is prescribed for the crime of theft and it is enhanced if the thief is a member of the upper caste. This is contrary to the prescription of punishment relating to other crimes. False evidence in disputes involving theft of property is viewed with seriousness. All these unmistakably prove that the smrti-kars by using both secular and theological deterrents, seek the preservation and safeguarding of private property.[70]

It has to be emphasized that in spite of many centuries having elapsed since the institution of private property came into being in ancient India, its suffocation within the narrow cell of communal society and tribal concepts continued an consequently property in land remained fettered in matters of free transferability. The Arthasastra of Kautilya states that kinsmen, neighbours and rich persons shall in succession go for the purchase of land and other holding. Brhaspati lays down that kinsmen whether united or separate are all alike

66. Gaut. DH. S. XII. 15.
67. *Ibid.*
68. *Ibid.*
69. *Ibid.*
70. *Ibid.*

as regards immovable property, and no one of them has power in any way to give, mortgage or sell it.[71] Katyayana concludes that there can be no lawful sale or purchase of land without securing approval of a kinsman of the seller and buyer. He prescribes the time limit, within which the kinsmen have the right to veto the transactions of sale made by a kinsman.[72] Kautilya lays down that taxpayers shall sell or mortgage their fields to tax payers alone. Brahamama shall sell or mortgage their brahmadeya or gifted lands only to those who are endowed with such lands.[73] The restrictions on alienation of property outside the kinships and the right given to the kinsmen to veto such an alienation of property outside the kinship is a clog on free alienation of property during our period. It indicates that property rights are still fettered with primitive restrictions. This fact is further corroborated by the complete absence of wills in the smrtis even though complicated rules are laid down to govern such transactions as interest, mortgage, etc. A will or testament is an instrument by which the devolution of an inheritance is prescribed, and as such it is a posthumous disposition. Through will a property holder is able to dispose of his property even after his death. The absence of wills therefore shows that landed property has not yet reached a stage of full and unfettered ownership with unrestricted rights to make alienations to anyone or at anytime (jusutendi et abutendi, i.e. the right of disposing of a thing at will).

The prevalence of fetters on right to property is not a feature conspicuous to ancient India alone, but conforms to the general pattern obtaining in all primitive societies where men are regarded and related not as individuals but always as members of a particular group. Their individuality is swallowed up in their family. Such a society has for its units not individuals but groups of men united by the reality[74] of the fiction of blood relationship. The institution of will was

71. *Ibid.*
72. Kat. 702-3.
73. AS, BK. III. Ch. X.
74. H.S. Maine, Ancient Law, p. 183.

unknown in Athens until the time of Solon.[75] Thc smrti law books stress that brothers, near relatives, bandhus, sakulyas, and his kinsmen all near or remote, have claim of inheritance to the property after the demise of a kinsman. Introduction of wills as a form to determine inheritance contained a real danger of giving a direct blow to the tribal organization and was likely to result in the property passing out of its hands. Under the circumstances it was natural for the smrti lawyers to introduce the clever device of the adoption of sons who on the one hand fulfil the requirements of oblation and lineage while of the other prevent the property from going into the hands of persons outside the gana or the extended family, for the adopted so was necessarily to become the member of the gana. Keeping in view this aspect of landed property it appears that although individuals or their families are assigned their separate areas of land and although these possessions have become hereditary, yet the rights seem to operate within the larger circle of gentile rights over these individual or family rights to property.

75. F. Engels, Origin of the Family, Private Property and State, Marx-Engels Selected Words, p. 294.

Chapter

10

Varna Legislation

The law-books enjoin upon all the members of the twice-born caste to study the Veda, to offer sacrifices for their own sake and to give alms.[1] Teaching, performing sacrifices for others and receiving alms are the occupations of a brahmana[2] in addition to the lawful occupations mentioned above.[3] To these Apastamba auds other lawful occupations such as inheriting, gleaning come in the field and living by taking the things which do not belong to anybody.[4] Gautama makes agriculture, trade and lending money at interest also lawful occupations for brahmana provided he does not do the work himself.[5] The last named three occupations of a brahmana are not prescribed by any other smrti.[6] Apastamba states that for a ksatriya the lawful occupations are the same as for a brahmana, but a ksatriya cannot teach, officiate as priest, and receive alms.[7] It is not clear whether he approves

1. Gaut. Dh. S. X.1; Manu, 1.88; X.75; Yaj. 1.118.
2. Gaut. Dh. S. X.2.
3. *Ibid.*, X.3.
4. Ap. Dh. S. 4.II.5.10, 4-5.
5. Gaut. Dh. S., X. 5-6.
6. SBE, Vol. II, Part I, p. 228, fns. 5-6.
7. Ap. Dh. S. 11.5.10.6; Cf. Manu, 1.89, X.77-79; Yaj. 1.119.

for the ksatriya also the gleaning of com in the fields and taking of other things belonging to nobody. He adds governing and fighting as occupations of a ksatriya.[8] The lawful occupation of a vaisya is the same as that of a ksatriya with the exception of governing and fighting which are the latter's prerogatives. Both Apastamba and Gautama assign, agriculture, tending of cattle and trade to vaisya.[9] Gautama declares that gain by labour is an additional mode of acquisition for a vaisya or sudra.[10] Sudras constitute the fourth-caste and are to seek their livelihood by serving the upper castes.[11] They are also permitted to live by practising various crafts.[12]

Among the castes the brahmanas are given a very elevated position. The king is advised to respect the brahmanas according to the sastra in order to please the subjects.[13] One of the important duties of the king is to worship the gods and brahmanas.[14] Brahmanas are the gods of gods, and whatever they say is fo. the welfare of all. Therefore, members of the other varnas should perform the yajus rituals according to the advice of the brahmanas and not on their own.[15] A brahmana deserves more respect than the king. The road belongs to the king except if he meets a brahmana, for in that case it belongs to a 'brahmana.[16] A ten year old brahmana is like a father to a hundred year old ksatriya.[17]

The law-books confer on the brahmanas many economic advantages. A learned brahmana is free from taxes.[18] Visnu lays down that the "king should not levy any

---

8. Ap. Dh. S. 11.5.10.7; Manu, 1.90; X.78.
9. Ap. Dh. S. 11.5.10.7; Gaut. Dh. S. X.42.
10. Gaut. Dh. S. X.42; Vas. Dh. S. 11.16.
11. Gaut. Dh. S. X.56-57; Vas. Dh. S. 11.20.
12. Gaut. Dh. S., X.60.
13. SP. 56.12.
14. *Ibid.*, 56.15; Visnu, 111.76.
15. SP. 60.43.
16. Ap. Dh. S. 11.5.11.6.
17. Ap. Dh. S. 1.4.14.25; Manu, II.135; Visnu, XXX, n. 17.
18. Ap. Dh. S. 11.10.26.10; Vas. Dh. S. XIX.23; Manu, VIII.394.

tax on the brahmanas for they pay taxes to him, in the shape of their pious acts."[19] A sixth part both of the virtuous deeds and of the iniquitous acts committed by his subjects go to the king.[20] As against the brahmanas, sudras are given the lowliest status in society. He has to serve the twice born castes, and under the smrti-laws has no identity of his own. He is to use the cast off shoes, umbrellas, garments and mats discarded in his favour by his master.[21] What is worse, a smrti-rule even goes to the extent of making it the responsibility of a sudra to maintain his master of -the higher caste if he falls into distress.[22] His accumulated savings are meant to serve this purpose.[23] Slavery is reserved for sudras. It is no crime for the mlechchas to sell or mortgage the life of their own offspring.[24] A sudra whether bought or unbought may be compelled to serve the twiceborn, for "he was created by the self-existent (Svaymbhu) to be the slave of the brahmana."[25] Even though he is emancipated by his master he is not released from servitude since that is innate in him.[26]

We cannot get a realistic picture of society, men and their material life in ancient times if we confine our investigation only to the superficial aspects of castes and social inequality. The smrtis and the other similar sources give considerable material to understand the more fund amental aspect of society. In the Arthasastra of Kautilya we get a picture of an absolute state where even the process of production is controlled and guided by the state. We nave the picture of house lands on which the slave labourers and others work under state supervision. Ploughs, bullocks, seed and other means of production are supplied to the workers

19. Visnu, III.26-27.
20. Vas. Dh. S. III.28.
21. Gaut. Dh. S. X.58.
22. *Ibid.*, X. 62.
23. *Ibid.*, X. 63.
24. AS. BK.II. Ch. XIII.
25. Manu, VIII.413.
26. Manu, VIII.414.

by the state, which takes the regular assistance of craftsmen such as blacksmiths, carpenters, rope makers, etc.[27] We may add that the Aryan society had merged out of its tribal stage and the individual's right of holding private property within the community was developing.

This does not mean that all productive activities were carried on by the state alone. We also come across cultivators who carried on agriculture on their own and paid to the state a fixed share of the produce.[28] According to the commentator the king is the owner of both land and water, and the people can exercise their right over all the other things excepting these two.[29] Jayaswal considers the theory of sovereign's proprietory right in land to be an impossibility. The king gets a sixth part of the produce and other shares of commodities not as 'royalty' not because it grows out of the land in the kingdom but because it is produced under the protection offered by him.[30] That the state was deemed to be the owner of all lands, was only a general proposition in the view of Kane. In his opinion where individuals or bodies of persons had been in long possessions of lands, ownership of the state was qualified and restricted only to the recovery of taxes and such individual and groups were regarded practically as owners of land, subject to payment of the tax and their eviction in case of default.[31]

Maity, however, basing himself on a host of Gupta inscriptions which require the ordinary citizens to obtain the royal permission for purchase and donation of land thinks that the king enjoyed supreme ownership right over the whole village, "otherwise he could not transfer such comprehensive rights over the whole village in such a way."[32]

Sufficient evidence has been mustered to prove beyond doubt that consistent with the injunctions laid down in the Dharmasastra, portions of the epics, the Anusasana Parva of

---

27. AS., BK.II. Ch. XXIV.
28. AS., BK.II. Ch. XXIV.
29. AS., BK.II, Ch. XXIV, fn. 5.
30. K.P. Jayaswal, Manu and Yaj., p. 105.
31. P.V. Kane, HDS, Vol. III, pp. 495-96.
32. S.K. Maity, Economic Life of Northern India in Period, p. 25.

the Mahabharata, the custom and practice of making land grants to brahmanas had grown to a significant scale in the post-Maurya period, a process which tended to feudalise the state apparatus.[33] Even the Arthasastra of Kautilya provides for the grant of brahmadeya lands yielding sufficient produce and exempted from the taxes and fines; it also provides for endowing of public servants with lands but no right to alienate the same by sale or mortgage.[34] Manu provides for the appointment of a lord over each village, as well as lords of the villages, lords of twenty, lords of a hundred and lords of 'thousand villages'.[35] The king should endow these rulers with land or revenues sufficient for their maintenance.[36]

According to Lalitavistara everyone of the thousands of kings in Vaisali had his own bhandagarika and his own store house, and must have his own landed property to fill the storehouse.[37] In view of the above it appears certain that the grants helped to create powerful intermediaries, wielding considerable economic and polittcal power.[38] From reference in the Arthasastra it appears that high born persons occupying land assumed such importance as to cause troubles for the state.[39]

CHANGING PATTERN OF CLASSES AND PROPERTY RELATIONS

In the Arthasastra of Kautilya we get a clear picture of a developing agriculture. Great attention is being paid to the regulation, development and extension of agriculture by the state. Excess population from the thickly populated entres are resettled in a new village. Even the foreigners are to be

33. R.S. Sharma, Indian Feudalism, p. 2.
34. AS., BK.II, Ch. 1.
35. Manu, VII.115.
36. *Ibid.*, VII.119.
37. Quoted by Walter Ruben "Some Problems of the Ancient Indian Republics," in KMA, p. 19.
38. R.S. Sharma, "Origin of Feudalism in India", in JESHO; Vol. I.3, pp. 299-300.
39. AS. BK. VIII. Ch. IV.

induced to form villages on new sites or on old ruins.[40] Unreclaimed, lands were given to persons for being cultivated, and a measure of safety was afforded to them. The state may have also developed lands for cultivation and then given away to cultivators. The rule in the Arthasastra that "lands prepared for cultivation shall be given to tax payers (karada) only for life (ekapursikani) suggests such a practice." The state might have found such a practice of preparing land for cultivation necessary on account of the lack of means, such as ploughs and other implements for breaking the virgin soil, on the part of new cultivators. Swelling of the treasury is the chief objective of the state and bringing of new areas under cultivation is a sure means to achieve this. With the same objective in view lands are to be confiscated from those who do not cultivate them and given to others.[41] On the other hand, if the cultivators pay their taxes easily, they may be favourably supplied with grain, cattle and money.[42] Only such favours and remissions are to be granted to the cultivators as tend to swell the treasury.[43] Remission of taxes is prescribed on the occasion of opening of new settlements,[44] perhaps to provide incentive for cultivators to settle down and work on the new settlement. Remission of tax is permitted in emergencies.[45] Obviously these mean floods, droughts and famines in which remission of taxes are provided to preserve the cultivating capacity and means of the cultivator for the ensuing seasons of cultivation.

In the Arthasastra we do not come across any clear reference to the lands given by individual to others for the purposes of cultivation. But a rule in Apastamba clearly indicates the leasing of lands by individual owners to tenants for cultivation. If a person has taken a lease of land for cultivation but does not exert himself, as a result of which

40. *Ibid.*, BK.II. Ch. I.
41. AS. BK.II. Ch. I.
42. *Ibid.*, BK.II. Ch. I.
43. *Ibid.*, BK.II. Ch. I..
44. *Ibid.*, BK.II. Ch. I.
45. *Ibid.*, BK.II. Ch. I.

the land bears no crops, he is to pay to the owner of the land the value of the crop that ought to have been grown by him.[46] Yajnavalkya mentions three stages in the system of land relationship, i.e. Mahipati (king); Ksatra Svami (land owner) and Krsaka (cultivator). If a cultivator after taking the land from the landowner (Svami) neither cultivates himself nor permits it to be cultivated by someone else, he is liable to pay again equivalent to that which ought to have been produced in the land and also to forfeit the land.[47] Brhaspati lays down that the cultivator who takes the ground on lease shall sow and water it and reap the harvest in due season. In the event of a failure on his part to perform these duties he is to be compelled to make good the average value of the crop to the owner.[48] According to Dr. Sharma these cultivators were temporary peasants.[49]

The smrti and the Arthasastra of Kautilya are alive to the problem-arising out of enjoyment of properties by persons having no title and have laid down rules relating to disputes arising out of this problem. The Arthasastra and Dharmasutras, however, nowhere mention clearly land as falling within this category of properties. Kautilya generally states that if the owner neglects for ten years ills property which is under the enjoyment of others, he shall forfeit his title to it.[50] According to Gautama the property of persons other than an idiot or a minor, if enjoyed by a stranger before his eyes for ten years, belongs to such a stranger.[51] He, however, clearly exempts animals, lands and women from the operation of this rule.[52]

Vasistha classifies the property inherited from a father, a thing bought; the property given to a wife after marriage

46. Ap. Dh. S. II. 11.2.8.
47. Yaj., II. 158.
48. Br. XIX. 29.
49. R.S. Sharma, "Economic Life and Organisation in Ancient India", p. 55.
50. AS., BK. III. Ch. XVI.
51. Gaut. Dh. S. XII. 37.
52. *Ibid.*, XII. 39.

by the husband's family, a gift, property obtained for performing a sacrifice, the property of the united coparceners and wages as eight types of properties which are lost to, the owner if they have been enjoyed by another person for ten years continuously.[53] The properties exempted. from the operation of this rule are a pledge, a boundary and the property of a minor, an open deposit, a sealed deposit, women, the property of king and the wealth of a srotriya.[54] Visnu however clearly states that if possession. of an estate has been held by three successive generations in due course, the fourth in descent shall keep it as his property, even without a written title.[55] Yajnavalkya lays down that if a stranger cultivates the land for twenty-years before the eyes of the owner who does not protest, the owner loses his ownership of such a property.[56] Further he says that written document is a more authoritative proof of title than possession enjoyed for three generations.[57] There appears to be a contradiction in the period prescribed by Yajnavalkya himself under these two rules. He considers only such possession as have written document as a proof of title, but at the same time he lays down that: where there is no element of possession, written document loses force.[58]

Narada, like his predecessors, lays down the principle that if goods are enjoyed by strangers before the owner's eyes, they shall belong to the stranger[59] and can not be recovered by him if he suffers such an enjoyment by the stranger for a period of ten years.[60] In spite of the acceptance of this principle of adverse possession he makes title necessary in order to establish proprietory right.[61] The person putting forward possession as his only claim to right is to be

53. Vas. Dh. S. XVI. 16.17.
54. *Ibid.*, XVI. 18; Manu, 149; Yaj. n. 25.
55. Visnu, V.187.
56. Yaj. 11.24.
57. *Ibid.*, 11.27.
58. Yaj. II.27.
59. Nar. I.78.
60. *Ibid.*, I.79.
61. *Ibid.*, I.84.

considered as a thief. He who enjoys without a title for even so many hundred years, the ruler or the land should inflict on that sinful man the punishment. Narada, however, contradicts himself when he lays down that when possession has been held unlawfully by the three ancestors of the father of the present possessor, the property can not be taken away from him because it has gone through three lives in order.[62] Brhaspati declares that possession held by three generations produced ownership for strangers when they are related[63] to one another in the degree of a sapinda; but makes this rule inapplicable to the Sakulyas.[64] He further adds that possession held by a relation, a friend, a relative or a kinsman does not disentitle an owner of a house, field, commodity or other property.[65] Thus while the former rule of Brhaspati (IX.I0) seeks to limit the right of adverse possession to a limited circle of sapindas, the later rule (IX.10) takes away this right from the relation, a friend, relative or a kinsman. Both these rules, however, further contradict another clear rule laid down by Brhaspati, namely that if one holds possession of an estate after having merely taken it, and occupies it without any resistance he becomes the legitimate owner of such an estate which is lost to the owner by such forbearance.[66] Among the smrti-writers the credit for clarity on the question of possession goes to Katyayana, who lays down that possession is of two sorts, with title and without title. Possession which continues for three generations is an independent means of proof of title, but if the possession is for less than three generations, it is a proof of ownership only when it is accompanied with title.[67] He ordains that the king or judges should not interfere with possession which is immemorial and not known to have originated without title.[68] Further when a person inherits from his father a property

62. *Ibid.*, I. 86-87.
63. *Ibid.*, I. 91.
64. Br., IX. 10.
65. *Ibid.*, IX. 11.
66. *Ibid.*, IX. 6.
67. Kat. 317.
68. *Ibid.*, 325.

which. has been enjoyed by the father according to the usual mode of enjoying the property, he should not, after the death ot the father, be called upon to prove his title.[69] When the land has been duly enjoyed by three generations the fourth secures ownership right over it even in the absence of documents.[70] He upholds the principle of law that a possession which is unbroken and of long standing (immemorial) is a strong and independently valid proof of title in law.[71]

The above examination of the principle of law laid down by the smrti-kars on the question of title and possession shows that the smrti-kars have not only been contracting each other, but more often than not themselves on vital points of possession and title. The growing divorce between ownership of land and actual use and possession must have given rise to an increasing number of disputes in the agrarian society of the period. In a period when uncultivated land was available in plenty, many individuals or families must have found it expedient with their growing numbers to clear forest or other lands and bring them under cultivation. The investment of physical labour and reasources in clearing such unclaimed lands, especially in a period when extension of agriculture was much encouraged, was supposed to confer upon the individual a lawful claim to this property.[72] This view gets ample support from the rule of Manu according to which the land belongs to him who first clears it and dear to him who first wounds up.[73]

The practice of making grants of considerable areas of land in far and near places to the brahmanas and other intermediaries introduced an element of property rights in land. It is reasonable to conclude that within the areas or villages so donated lay many such lands as were cleared by individuals and were cultivated, possessed and enjoyed by

69. Kat. 320.
70. *Ibid.*, 327.
71. *Ibid.*, 329.
72. *Ibid.*, 329.
73. Manu, IX. 44.

them as owners. The question that arises is as to how was the conflict between the powerful grantees, both secular and religious who derived their titles from the royal grants, and the peasants who derived their titles through reclamation and possession, resolved? The possibility of such a conflict between the *defacto* and the *dejure* owners perhaps: explains Manu's rule that the acceptance by a brahmana of a gift of an untilled land is less blamable than that of a tilled one.[74] The acceptance by a brahmana of a gift of tilled land is bound to encroach upon the rights of the persons who are tilling such lands and may lead to conflicts between him and such tillers.

In the conflict between the landowners who have title to the land and the a dual cultivators who possess and cultivate it, the smrti laws appear to be invariably inclined to uphold the claims of title against those of possessions as: can be inferred from the above rules. Even after accepting the principle of adverse possession the Dharmasutras do not include land, the vital property, among the properties to be covered by this rule. Later works, while incorporating land in this category of property, suffer from so many contradictions that it is difficult to believe that the actual possessors could have the benefit of law in their favour against the title-owing landowner. Even when the later smrti-kars of the Gupta period such as Brhaspati and Katyayana accept possession as a source of title, they make the duration of such possession very long, i.e. three to four generations. In view of this the conclusion appears to be incontrovertible that tenants of longstanding could be displaced from the fields by the secular and religious grantees if there was even a short break in their tenancy or occupancy.[75] Since it is very difficult to prove possession over long periods of three or four generations, the position even of those cultivators whose ancestors first cleared the lands and began as *res nullius* possessor owner of their lands may have been rendered insecure in view of the laws of possession enunciated in the smrtis.

74. *Ibid.*, X. 114.
75. R.S. Sharma, Indian Feudalism, p. 150.

BRAHMANAS

As a result of the gifts of land made by kings, brahmanas emerged as a powerful class of property owners in society. The Arthasastra prescribes that those performing sacrifices (rtvik), spiritual guides, priests and men learned in the Vedas, should receive grants of brahmadeya lands yielding sufficient produce and exempt from taxes and fines.[76] The Dharmasutras and smrtis recommend the grant of lands to the brahmanas. As time passed large areas of land were granted to the brahmanas. This is fully established by a number of epigraphical records showing grant of lands, and villages by the kings to the brahmanas from time to time and in almost every region of the country.

Receiving of grants including gifts of lands is consistent with the traditional views on the lawful occupation of brahmanas as laid down in the smrtis and other texts. The smrti-kars, however, introduced significant changes in the lawful occupations of brahmanas. Gautama makes agriculture and trade also lawful for a brahmana provided he does not do the work himself.[77] A brahmana is also permitted to lend money at interest.[78] Thus, these rules allow brahmanas to be the gentleman farmers and sleeping partners in mercantile or banking business, managed by vaisyas.[79] It appears that many brahmanas adopted the pursuit of agriculture to earn a living for themselves. There was an inevitable conflict between the pursuit of agriculture and the study of Vedas, an important duty of brahmana caste. Baudhayana states that the study of the Veda impedes the pursuit of agriculture and *vice versa*. Those who are able to do both are permitted to attend to both of these pursuits, but not those who are unable to do both. Baudhayana recommends discarding the pursuit of agriculture in favour of the study of the Vedas.[80] A rule of

---

76. AS. BK. II. Ch. 1.
77. Gaut. Dh. S., X. 5.
78. *Ibid.*, X. 6.
79. George Bvihler, SBE, Vol. II, Part II, p. 228, fn.
80. Bjlud. Dh. S. I. 5.10.30.

Baudhayana suggests that brahmanas could plough the fields under certain restrictions such as yoking only those bulls whose noses had not been pierced and without striking them with the goad.[81]

Lending money at interest is also made lawful for a brahmana.[82] Brahmanas are allowed at their pleasure to lend money at interest to persons of certain categories.[83] The pursuits of agriculture, trade and money lending have been traditionally prescribed as the lawful occupation of vaisyas. The smrti-kars permitted these occupations to the brahmanas on the ground of a failure of the occupation lawful for a brahmana.[84] The departures from the lawful occupation is permitted during the times of distress (apat). Although trade is not lawful for a brahmana, he may, in times of distress, trade in lawful merchandise, avoiding the forbidden kinds.[85] He is allowed to sell various kinds of grains excepting sesamum or rice, provided he has not grown them himself.[86] Trading in lawful merchandise not bought by a brahmana is also permitted.[87] Vasistha permits a brahmana and a ksatriya a vaisya mode of living, with restrictions on the sale of certain commodities.[88] Narada accepts the occupations of a vaisya for a brahmana with restrictions to sell a number of articles.[89] But he permits the brahmanas to sell dry woog and dry grass, twigs of bomboo having fallen sponaneously, fruits of jujube tree, ropes and threads of cotton.[90]

What was the compelling factor which made the smrtikars introduce this drastic departure in the mode of livelihood of the brahmanas? The explanation offered for this in the smrtis is that such a provision is made to cope with a

81. *Ibid.*, II. 2.4.20-21.
82. Gaut. Dh. S. X. 6.
33. Baud. Dh. S. 1.5.10.25; Vas. Dh. S., II.
84. Gaut. Dh. S. VII.6.
85. Manu, X. 82-83.85. Ap. Dh. S. I. 7.20. 10-11.
86. Ap. Dh. S., I. 7.20.13.
87. *Ibid.*, I. 7.20.16.
88. VIII. Dh. S. II. 24.
89. Nar., I. 61-62.
90. *Ibid.*, 64-65.

situation of distress (apat). This leads us to another question. What was the nature and genesis of the distress which compelled the smrti-kars to declare the pursuit of vaisyas: as lawful for the brahamin? The attention given to this subject by all the smrti-kars from Gautama to Katyayana suggest that the situation of distress faced by the members of the brahmana caste was not negligible or insignificant, but had become widespread and assumed serious proportions inviting the attention of the lawgivers and compelling them to make suitable changes in the orthodox views regarding the lawful occupation of the brahmanas.

Another conclusion appears to be that all the members of the brahmana caste did not enjoy the same economic status. True, brahmanas were the recipients of gifts of lands and other valuables, but all the members of the brahmana caste could not have been in the same position with regard to receiving of favours from the kings or other members of the privileged nobility. This must have resulted in growing economic differences among the members of the brahmana caste itself. Along with grants of large estates to brahmanas we come across donations of ten or twelve dinaras for the maintenance of the brahmanas belonging to the community of perpetual alms house.[91] It may be inferred from Apastamba Dharmasutra that it was no longer possible for the brahmanas to subsist by the six lawful occupations prescribed for them, as he mentions gleaning corn in the field and taking other things belonging to nobody has additional lawful occupations of the brahmanas.[92] In spite of this, provision for times of distress are made whereby brahmanas are allowed to resort to the occupation of agriculture and trade. With the growth of population of both the brahmanas, and the other castes, the scope for subsistence by gleanings and taking of things belonging to nobody must have dwindled considerably making the distress of brahmanas more acute and general. Katyayana even permits a brahmana to do the work of an inferior kind if given by a brahmana although he forbids him

91. CII, III. No. 7, p. 39; CII, No. 8, p. 40; CII, III. No. 9, p. 41.
92. Ap. Dh. S. II. 5.10.4-5.

to do impure work.[93] According to Narada impure work is done by slaves while pure work is done by labourers.[94] According to this interpretation the brahmanas are permitted by Katyayana to serve their castemen even as labourers. It is thus clear from the reading of the smrtis that members of the brahmana caste though superior as a social and ritual groups were not economically of the same status. Economic changes and the growth of property relations caused class differentiations and economic inequalities among the member of the brahmana caste itself, rendering the economic condition of at least some of its members very much inferior to that or others belonging to their own caste.

The provision permitting the brahmanas to adopt the occupations of the ksatriyas and vaisyas must have led to the undermining of the economic position of the vaisyas. All the members of the twice-born caste are allowed, in times of distress, to adopt the occupations of the castes other than their own. It is, however, significant that persons unable to live by their own lawful occupations could adopt the occupation of the next inferior castes, but under no circumstances could they adopt the occupations of the higher castes.[95] As against this view we have an epigraphic record which states that members of a silkweaving community in Dasapura took to such occupations and pursuits. Such a provision in the smrti laws exposed the members of all the castes excepting brahmanas to the danger of competition from the members of their superior castes.[96] So far brahmanas are concerned this law provided them with complete immunity from competition by others in matters of their lawful occupations. The ksatriyas also appear not to have been affected adversely on account of this law. Although according to Baudhayana a brahmana unable to subsist by teaching, sacrificing for others or accepting of gifts shall maintain himself by following the duties of ksatriya,[97] he states the

93. Kat. 719.
94. Nar. V. 5.
95. Vas. Dh. S. II. 22; Visnu, II. 15.
96. CII III. 18. pp. 8-41.
97. Baud. Dh. S. II. 2.4.16.

contradictory view of Gautama forbidding for the brahmana the duties of a ksatriya on the ground that they are too cruel for a brahmana.[98] Ultimately Baudhayana allows the brahmana the livelihood of a vaisya because it is next to the ksatriya.[99] Thus the members of the vaisya caste must have suffered the full incidence of the inroads into their livelihood from the growing numbers of the higher castes unable to subsist by their own traditional occupations prescribed by law. In the social order members of the brahmana and ksatriya castes enjoyed considerable privileges which ensured them several advantages over the members of the vaisya caste even in such oocupations as agriculture, trade, money-lending, etc. Certain restrictions imposed on the brahmanas should not, however, be overlooked in this connection. A brahmana is not permitted to trade in certain kinds of forbidden articles.[100] He is not alloys to sell even rice or sesamum.[101] He is not to sell things after buying them.[102] Narada does not permit the brahmanas to sell milk, sour milk, clarified butter, honey, bees wax, lac, pungent condiments, liquids used for flavouring, spirituous liquor, meat, boiled rice, sesamum, linen, juice of Soma plant, flower, paint, precious stones, men, poison, weapons, water, salt cakes, plants, etc.[103] The Santi Parva forbids the sale of meat, wine, honey, salt, sesamum, cooked food, horse, oxen, cows, goats, sheep and buffaloes.[104] The restrictions put on the brahmana relating to the sale of these articles must have somewhat mitigated the hardships caused to the vaisyas on account of the influx of brahmanas into their occupations. It will, however, be clear that the forbidden articles bear the nature of ancillary to the main pursuit of agriculture. So far the realisation of the benefits of agriculture is concerned, the entry of the brahmanas must have had the inevitable effect of

98. *Ibid.*, II. 2.4.17; Gaut. Dh. S. VII. 6.
99. *Ibid.*, II. 2.4.19.
100. Ap. Dh. S., 1.7.20.10; Vas., Dh. S. II. 24.
101. Ap. Dh. S., 1.7.20.13; VII. Dh. S. 11.31; Manu, X. 19.
102. Ap. Dh. S., 1.7.20.16.
103. Nar. I. 61-62.

injuring seriously the economic position of the vaisyas as a class, pushing them nearer to the status of the sudras. Thus the law relating to distress for the vaisyas, who had no alternative but to take to the occupations of sudras and to live, as Manu ordains, by serving the members of the twice-born castes.[105] Thus the distinctions between the functions of the vaisyas and the sudras were being obliterated.[106]

SLAVERY AND SUDRAS

The Dharmasutras and smrtis assign to the sudras the role of service to the members of three higher castes. Apastamba asks the sudras to serve the other three castes and says that higher the caste he serves, greater is his merit.[107] He is to serve the higher Icastes and to seek his livelihood from them.[108] He shall use their cast off shoes, umbrellas, garments, and mats and eat the remnants of their food.[109] "One occupation only the lord prescribed to the sudra to serve meekly even these (other) three castes."[110] To serve the brahmanas learned in tke Vedas, and householders is the highest duty of a sudra and it leads to beatitude.[111] If a sudra is pure, gentle in his speech and free from pride he attains in his next life a higher caste.[112] The king is to order a sudra to serve the twice-born castes.[113] Yajnavalkya also lays down for a sudra the duty of serving the twice-born and in the event of his inability to live by this he may become a trader or adopt various acts, promoting the good of the twiceborn.[114] Gautama also allows the sudra to practise mechanical arts.[115]

104. SP., 78.5.
105. Manu, X. 98.
106. R.S. Sharma, Sudras in Ancient India, p. 177.
107. Av. Dh. S. 1.1.1.7-8
108. Gaut. Dh. S. X. 56-57.
109. *Ibid.*, X. 58-59.
110. Mann, 1. 91.
111. *Ibid.*, IX. 334.
112. *Ibid.*, IX. 335.
113. *Ibid.*, VT IIA 10.
114. Yij., X. 20.
115. Gaut. Dh. S. X. 60.

While the sudras were socially the lowest and vilest sections of society they were economically very important for carrying on production. We have already seen in the Arthasastra of Kautilya the efforts to set-up new villages and open up new areas of cultivation with the help of the sudra families.[116] The superintendent of agriculture is to employ slaves, labourers and prisoners to sow the seeds on the crown lands.[117] The agricultural operations are not allowed to be hampered for want of necessary means of production, such as ploughs, buffaloes, etc. and for this reliance is placed on the assistance of blacksmiths, carpenters, bores, rope-makers and others. These appear to be men of sudra caste who are permitted, as seen earlier to adopt the mechanical arts. Here we have a clear indication of the fact that sudras were employed on a large scale as slaves and hired labourers to carry on agricultural operations. Kautilya indicates that the sudras engaged in agricultural operation had two different relationships with land. The sudras working on the state farms were mere slaves devoid of means of production, such as land, ploughs, bullocks, seed, etc. these were provided to them by the superintendent of agricultre. On the other hand Kautilya devises the method of pushing out the excessive populations from the thickly populated centres and founding new villages having hundred to five hundred families of agricultural people of sudra caste. Lands are to be given to the tax payers for cultivation.[118] Even foreigners are to be induced to immigrate and settle down on the new sites or on the old ruins,[119] It appears that during this period there was great need as well as scope for the extension of agriculture to new areas and regions. But the population was relatively insufficient for the task. The specific provisions contained in Kautilya's Arthasastra relating to the duty of the king state that orphans be provided with maintenance, the afflicted and the helpless as well as women who are carrying be looked

---

116. AS, BK. n. Ch. I.
117. IbM, BK. n. Ch. XXIV.
118. AS, BK. n. Ch. I.
119. *Ibid.*, BK.II. Ch. I.

after. This concern may have arisen on account of the realisation of the importance of a larger population.[120] No person is allowed to embrace asceticism without making provision for the maintenance of his wife and sons nor is the conversion of a woman to asceticism permitted.[121] The desirability of having an increased population weighed heavily in the mind of the author of the Arthasastra is amply clear from the rule which permits one to become ascetic only after one has become incapable of producing children.[122] No wonder the gopas or the village (headmen) are to ascertain the total number of men and beasts as well as the causes of emigration and immigration of persons of a migratory nature.[123] An account has to be kept of the exact number of cultivators, cowherds, merchants, atisans, labourers, slaves, and biped and quadruped animals.[124]

From the above it appears that during the Maurya period the paucity of population had itself become a single important economic factor necessitating a shift of reliance from slaves to tenants for agriculture giving several incentives for cultivation. According to Dr. Sharma the sudras along with the vaisya peasants performed the role of the primary producers and thus provided the material foundations for the growth of the society. As agricultural labourers they helped to open to cultivation the thickly wooded areas of Kosala and Magadha. We do not have sufficient materials to form a correct idea about the proportion of the lands worked with the help of slaves and hired labourers or by the tenants. The only definite conclusion we can have with some amount of certainty is that the process of transformation of sudra from the position of slaves and hired labourers into that of agriculturists had started during the Mauryan period, a process which developed fully during the Gupta and post-Gupta period.[125] In the Arthasastra there are fields which are

---

120. *Ibid.,* BK.II. Ch. I.
121. *Ibid.,* BK.II. Ch. I.
122. *Ibid.,* BK.II. Ch. I.
123. *Ibid.,* BK.II. Ch. XXXV.
124. *Ibid.,* BK.II. Ch. XXXV.
125. R.S. Sharma, Sudras in Ancient India, p. 101.

left unsown (Vapatiriktam) owing to the inadequacy of hands, and reliance is placed on employing those who cultivate forhalf the share in the produce (ardhasirika) or on those who live by their own physical exertion.[126] The smrtis contain increasing number of references to sharecropping tenants.

Slavery and sudras do not appear to be co-extensive denominations as slavery was not exclusively confined to the sudras. According to Dr. Sharma the earliest identification of the sudras with the slave is found in an early Pali text and not in the Dharmasutras where it can be inferred only indirectly. According to Narada slavery is not ordained in the inverse order of the four castes. But this: rule does not apply to cases where a man violates duties peculiar to his caste.[127] A perusal of the seven kinds of slaves do not appear to include only the sudras in the category of slaves.[128] According to Manu the slaves are of seven kinds, i.e. one who is made a captive, one who serves for his daily food, one who is born in the house, one who is bought and one who is given, one who is inherited and one who is enslaved.[129] In contrast to these seven kinds of slaves Narada enumerates as many as fifteen by adding eight more categories as those who are maintained during a general famine, who are pledged by their rightful owners, who are released from heavy debts, who are owned through a wager, who offer themselves declaring "I am thine", who are apostate from ascenticism, who are enslaved on account of their connection with women slaves and who are self sold.[130] Although during the period between Manu and Narada there is marked increase in the types of slaves, yet it would be wrong to conclude that between these two periods employment of slave labour had grown. Narada himself states that slaves do impure work and enumerates such works as are done by slaves.[131]

---

126. AS. BK. n. Ch. XXIV.
127. Nar. V. 39; Yaj. II. 183.
128. Manu, V. 415.
129. Manu, VIII. 415.
130. Nar. V. 26-28.
131. *Ibid.*, V. 6-7.

None of the duties assigned to the slaves, has anything to do with the process of production or agriculture, which clearly underlines the fact that by the time of Narada; slavery had ceased to exist as a mode of production. Earlier even Manu and Visnu place one's labourer or sharecropper and slave among the sudras whose food the owner may eat.[132] The above references which treat the sharecropper or the agricultural labourer separately show that slave labourer was no longer employed in agricultural operations, which were carried on either by hired labourer or sharecroppers, and sudras were given land on lease for which they paid a share of the produce in return.

SHARECROPPERS

The king had a share in the produce of the land, and the smrtis recognised this royal right. According to Gautama cultivators must pay to the king a tax amounting to one eighth or one-sixth of the produce.[133] Visnu fixes a sixth part of the grain for the king every year as well as a sixth part of all the other seeds. Kautilya especially prescribes the proportion of the produce to be collected from such cultivators who use irrigation.[134] This water rate increases with the increasing efficacy of the mode of irrigation applied.[135] Thus one who irrigates by manual labour is to pay one-fifth of the produce, one who uses water lifts one-third and one who raises water from river, hikes, tanks and well one-third or one-fourth of the produce.[136] As regards the general rate of tax "it appears that one-sixth of the produce was levied by the king on the cultivator."[137]

The smrtis do not give detailed references to the taxes to be paid to the king. But the relationship between the land-owner on the one hand and the sharecropper and agricultural

132. Manu, IV. 253; Visnu; LVII. 16; Yaj., 1.166.
133. Gaut. Dh. S., X. 24.
134. Visnu, III. 22-23; Nar. XVIII. 48.
135. AS. BK. III, Ch. IX.
136. AS. BK. II, Ch. XXIV.
137. AS. BK. II, Ch. XV.

servants on the other receives greater attention. This may perhaps be on account of the fact that while the Arthasastra the sharecropper received land from the state, he did so in the smrtis from individual owners.[138] Brhaspati refers to two kinds of sharecroppers.

Those belonging to the first category receive food and clothing from the owner and take a fifth of the crop, others belonging to the second category work in consideration of profit alone and take a third part of the grain produce.[139] Dr. Sharma infers from the existence of the latter and of sharecropper the rise of a new stratum of labourers who possessed resources to meet their requirements.

Agricultural Servants

The smrtis refer to agricultural labourers working for wages and seek to regulate the relationship between master and servant by laying down rules.[140] According to Yajnavalkya if the master employs servants, without stipulating his wages, in trade, cattle rearing or agriculture, they shall be paid by the master one-tenth of the gains arising out of these occupations.[141] A master shall regularly pay wages to the servant hired by him as per the agreement.[142] Where wages have not been fixed the servant of a trader, a herdsman and an agricultural servant is to be paid a tenth part of the profit derived from the sale of the merchandise, of the seed, of cows and of the grain respectively.[143] Katyayana also prescribes as wages of a tenth part of the profits to such servants.[144] Dr. Sharma holds that towards the end of the Gupta period the wages of agricultural labourers were doubled.[145]

---

138. R.S. Sharma, Sudras in Ancient India, p. 217.
139. Br. XVI. 12-13.
140. R.S. Sharma, Sudras in Ancient India, p. 277.
141. Yaj. II. 194.
142. Nar. VI. 2.
143. *Ibid.*, VI. 3.
144. Kat. 656.
145. R.S. Sharma, Sudras in Ancient India, p. 227.

The smrtis draw heavily from the rules in Kautilya's Arthasastra relating to the fulfilment of the duties by the servants engaged in agriculture. The Arthasastra prescribes fine for the servant who receives wages but neglects unreasonably puts off the work. He is to be caught hold of till the work is done.[146] A cultivator who arrives at a village for work but does not work, is to be fined. He has to refund not only twice the amount of the wages he received while promising to work but also to return double the value of food and drink with which he may have been provided. Apastamba prescribes flogging for a servant in village who abandons his work, the same punishment is provided for a negligent herdsman.[147] Visnu prescribes that a hired workman who abandons his work before the expiry of the term should pay the whole amount of stipulated wages to his employer and also one hundred panas to the king as fine.[148] Manu states that a hired servant or workman, who, without being ill, fails to perform out of pride his work according to the agreement shall be fined, eight Krishnalas and no wages shall be paid to him.[149]

Yajnavalkya lays down that when a servant receives the wages but abandons the work he shall be made to pay double the amount of the wages to the master. If the assigned work is abandoned without his having received the: wages he shall be made to pay the amount of the wages to the master.[150] Brhaspati states that if a servant fails in the performance of even a small part of his master's work he forfeits his wages and makes himself liable to be sued[151] in court for his offence;[152] if he does not perform the work after having received his wages he is to be compelled to pay twice the amount of the wages as fine to the king and to return the wages to his master. The use of forcible means is prescribed

146. AS. BK. IV, Ch. 1.
147. Ap. Dh. S. II. 11.28.23.
148. Visnu, IV. 153.
149. Manu, VIII. 215.
150. Yaj., II. 193.
151. Nar., VI. 5.
152. Br., XVI. 14.

to compel the servant to do the work he promised to do. If the work is neglected on account of obstinacy on the part of the servants, he is to be fined eight Krishnalas, and payment of his wages is withheld.[153]

Katyayana states that if a servant begins the work but does not finish it he should be forced by the king. Such a servant deserves to be fined if he does not do the work.[154] Similar coercive measures are also prescribed for dealing with herdsman. Apastamba provides that the cattle should be replaced or any equivalent payment be made by the owner by the herdsmen if the cattle perishes or get lost because of his negligence.[155] If the cattle is attacked by wolves or other ferocious animals during day time and the keeper does not go to repel the attack, he shall have to make good to the owner the value of the cattle that has perished.[156] Manu and Narada lay downing similar rules.[157]

Yajnavalkya makes it the duty of the cowherd to return the cattle to the owner in the same conditions as the owner had handed them over to him. In the event of any loss on account of negligence the owner may withhold his salary and recover the price of the cattle.[158] The cowherd is also to pay a fine of thirteen and half panas if the cattle perishes on account of his fault.[159]

The above rules regarding the relationship between the master and servant, payment of wages, fulfilment of the contract of work, and use of compulsions such as fine, floggings and coercion show the anxiety of the smrti law-givers to ensure that the hired servants and herdsmen did not neglect or abandon their work. In case they did so the smrti laws provided sufficient justification and a legal basis of the landowners, masters, and cattle owners to use the severe

---

153. *Ibid.*, XVI. 16.
154. Kat. 657.
155. Ap. Dh. S., II. 11.28.6.
156. Visnu, V. 137.
157. Manu, VIII. 232; Nar., V. 14. 3
158. Yaj. II. 164.
159. *Ibid.*, II. 165.

punishments prescribed in law and thus keep the wage labourers and herdsmen under control.

CLASSES AND THE STATE

"The smrtis clearly emphasize the crucial role of the state" symbolised by the king in the preservation of society. Gautama makes it the duty of the king to protect all human beings, to inflict lawful punishments, to support the brahmanas, ksatriyas, to collect taxes and to protect the taxpayers.[160] Governing and fighting is the occupation of the ksatriya, according to Apastamba.[161] The king should protect his subjects receiving as his pay a sixth part of their income or spiritual merit.[162] The ksatriyas are endowed with strength together with duties and privileges of using weapons, and protecting the treasure and the life of created beings for the growth of good government.[163] Vasistha says that it is the peculiar duty of the ksatriya, to protect the people with his weapons and that he is togain his livelihood from this occupation.[164] A ksatriya is to reiform his obligation of constant practice in arms,[165] and to protect the world and receive due regard in the form of taxes.[166] The royal duties include protection of his people,[167] keeping the four castes and the four orders in the practice of the several duties,[168] and to appoint chiefs or governors and lords to administer the villages and districts.[169] God commanded the ksatriya to protect the. people.[170] He must duly protect the whole world.[171] The king has been created to be the protector of the

160. Gaut. Dh. S., X. 7.8.9. 24-27.28.
161. Ap. Dh. S., II. 5.10.6.
162. Baud. Dh. S., 1.10.18.1.
163. Baud. Dh. S., 1.10.18.3.
164. Vas. Dh. S. II. 17.
165. Visnu, II. 6.
166. *Ibid.*, II. 12.
167. *Ibid.*, III. 2.
168. *Ibid.*, III. 3.
169. *Ibid.*, III. 8-15; Manu, VII. 114-117.
170. Manu, I. 89.
171. *Ibid.*, VII. 3.

castes (varna) and orders, all of whom discharge their several duties according to their ranks.[172]

The smrtis enunciate the principles which clearly indicate that the work of government and administration was in reality not the exclusive domain of the ksatriyas as a caste. The brahmanas appear, according to the smrtis, to wield considerable power and occupy important position in the field of government and administration which is ostensibly in the hands of the king or the ksatriyas. The state and government are based on a coalition of the brahmanas and ksatṛiyas. A king and a brahmana deeply versed in the Vedas uphold the moral order in the world.[173] On them depends the existence of the four-fold human race of eternally conscious beings, of those which move on feet and on wings, and of those which creep. On them also depends the protection of off-spring, the prevention of the confusion of the castes and the sacred law,[174] Gautama quotes the Veda, "Ksatriyas who are assisted by Brahmanas, prosper and do not fall into distress."[175] "Brahmanas united with. Ksatriyas, uphold gods, women and men."[176] The Santi Parva explains the evil consequences of a conflict between ksatriya and brahmana and points out that the ksatriya becomes miserable or weak when he comes into conflict with brahmana. As such the king is advised to bow down to the brahmana.[177] When king and purohita (brahmana) maintain cordiality and identical hearts they together bring prosperity to their subjects.[178] Only when brahmanas and ksatriyas remain united are they able to protect each other. Ksatriya is the foundation of the prosperity of brahmana, and the brahmana of the ksatriya.[179]

The important concessions and extraordinary privileges enjoyed by the brahmanas show their important position in

---

172. *Ibid.*, VII. 35.
173. Gaut. Dh. S., VIII. 1.
174. *Ibid.*, VIII. 2-3.
175. *Ibid.*, XI. 14.
176. *Ibid.*, IX. 27.
177. SP. 56.25-26.
178. *Ibid.*, 73.3-4.
179. *Ibid.*, 115.16.

the state. The king has right to take away the property of the subjects, but he is ordained not to touch the estate of a brahmana; the property of a brahmana is a terrible poison which, if taken destroys not only the person who takes it but also his sons and grandsons.[180] In matters of authority the word of brahmana is declared to be the highest law: "What Brahmanas, riding in the chariot of law (and) wielding the sword of the Veda, propound even in jest, is declared to be the highest law."[181] The brahmanas are the custodians of the Vedas and traditions as well as the competent authority to interpret the texts. True, with the progress of time and particularly during Maurya period the importance of king grew considerable. Katyayana gives the king the power to legislate, but this legislation is not to be opposed to dharma or sacred law.[182] Perhaps this sharing of state power is responsible for the dwarfing or checking the growth of royal legislation in ancient India. Even though the Moryan kings assumed to some degrees a legislative function yet they were always restricted on account of the necessity of harmonising the royal edict with the customary and sacred law.[183] This again explains the absence in ancient India of the justification of the doctrine that law is a command of a determinate political superior to an inferior enforced by sanction. The element of command was certainly not unknown in ancient India, for according to the Mimamsasutra of Jaimini dharma or duty is that which being discernible is indicated by the Vedic injunction. This injunction was however not the command of a political inferior. It emanated from a source which was superior to both and equally binding upon all. Dharma as enunciated in the Vedas and traditions, and interpreted by the learned brahmanas was above the king also and treated him in the same manner as it did the ordinary man. Since the brahmanas had the monopoly of studying and authoritatively interpreting the Vedas and

180. Vas. Dh. S., XVII. 84-86; 1.5.11.16.
181. Baud. Dh. S. 1.1.1.1-3.
182. Kiat., 38, 44; Manu, 3.
183. Drekmeir, Kingship and Community in Early India, p. 234.

traditions they had an edge over the k..g himself, who was duty bound under the smrti-laws to conform to dharma in matters both religious and secular.

Brahmanas and ksatriyas are the two highest castes in the social order. None of these two castes are assigned the sole of active participation in the field of production, trade or rearing of cattle, which are the mainstay of the material life and economic progress of the community. In the division of labour prescribed for the different castes in the Vedas and smrtis the vaisyas and sudras are to adopt the occupation of agriculture, trade, labour and service and earn their livelihood thereby. Thus we find in the smrtis the existence of a class of privileged persons belonging to the brahmana and ksatriya castes and not participating in the process of production. Even when brahmana is permitted to undertake agriculture and trade he is forbidden to work himself.[184] In contrast to this class of privileged persons we find the class of the tirtha people belonging to the vaisyas and sudras. Members of these vaisya caste engage themselves in agriculture, undertake cultivation of lands either belonging to themselves or to the landowner or the king, rear cattle, and also perform the task of exchange in society through trade and commerce. The sudras, besides rendering personal service to the members of the higher castes, perform the work of tilling, of ploughing the fields, irrigating it, reaping the harvests, etc. On the surplus produced by the toiling sections, the king, his army officers, etc. The cultivators belonging to these two lower classes and castes of society may pay to the king as tax a portion of the produce,[185] of cattle and gold,[186] of merchandise,[187] of roots and fruits, flowers, medicinal juice, meat, grass and lire wood.[188] The king is to live on surplus.[189] An artisan according to the smrtis is to do one day's work for

184. Gaut. Dh. S. X. 5.
185. *Ibid.*, X. 24; V. Manu, 22.
186. Gaut. Dh. S. X.25; Visnu, III. 24.
187. Gaut. Dh. S. X. 26.
188. Gaut. Dh. S. X. 27; Visnu, III. 25.
189. Gaut. Dh. S. X. 30.

the king.[190] The villagers have to furnish daily to the king such articles as food, drink and fuel through the lord of the village.[191] The king is to receive an eighth, sixth or twelfth part of the crops, and a fiftieth part of the increments on cattle and gold.[192] The king's share also includes a sixth part of trees, meat, honey, clarified butter, perfumes, medicinal herbs, substances used for flavouring food, flowers, roots and fruits, leaves, pot herbs, grass, objects made of cane, skin of earthen vessels and all articles made of stone.[193]

The privileged classes, the king, brahmanas, nobility, officialdom and others lived on such surplus created by the members of the toiling classes belonging to vaisya and sudra castes. The smrti lawgivers appear to be conscious of this sharp economic inequality between the different segments of society. The social order which makes one set of the privileged persons belonging to the brahmanas and ksatriya class live by the appropriation of the surplus produced by the labour of another set of working population must be its very nature be a social order of conflicting classes, castes and groups, interests and always fraught with the danger of chaos, confusion and collapse due to its internal strains and struggles. It is a serious concern of the smrtis to maintain the *status quo* of such a society and ensure the continuation of the system in vogue. Such a society can be maintained only when all the members fulfil the duties of their castes as laid down in the Vedas and traditions. The smrtis adopt two methods for achieving the objective, the methods of persuasion and those of coercion. The preservation of dharma (law), is of crucial importance for this objective. Dharma is the ksatra of ksatra; therefore, there is nothing higher than dharma; thus, even a weak man rules the stronger with the help of dharma as with the help of a king.[194] Sacred law (dharma) is based on the rule of conduct, and the lawgivers

190. *Ibid.*, X. 31; Visnu, III. 32; Vas. Dh. S., XIX. 28.
191. Manu, VII. 118.
192. *Ibid.*, VII. 130.
193. *Ibid.*, VII. 131-132.
194. Brihadaranyaka Upanisad, 1.4.14.

consider good conduct to be the most excellent rule of all austerity.[195]

Even austerity, study of the Veda and lavish liberality cannot save one whose conduct is vile and who has strayed from the path of duty.[196] Through good conduct a man gain spiritual merit as well as wealth.[197] Following the rule of conduct is doubtlessly the highest duty of all men.[198] Vatsyayana considers dharma to be superior to artha, and artha to kama.[199] A person who follows the precepts of sacred law and practices them, enters the universal soul.[200] Men of all castes enjoy in heaven the highest imperishable bliss when they fulfil their assigned duties.[201] When a man who has fulfilled his duties returns to this world, he obtains birth in a distinguished family, beauty of complexion, strength, aptitude for learning, wisdom, wealth and gift fulfilling the laws of his caste and order. In both the worlds he dwells in happiness.[202] It is the highest duty of all men to live according to the rule of conduct.[203] The rule of conduct is transcendent law whether it be taught in the revealed text or in the sacred tradition. A twice-born man, therefore; should always be careful to follow it if he has regard for himself.[204] If he persists in discharging the prescribed duties in the right manner he reaches the deathless state and even in this life obtains the fulfilment of all the desires that he may have conceived.[205] The path of the salvation of the lower castes, the sudras, is to be found in the zealous discharge of the duties earmarked for them. Apastamba seeks to impress upon these men particularly when he lays down that the successive births men of lower castes are born in the next higher one, if they fulfil their

195. Manu, I. 110.
196. Vas. Dh. S., VI. 2.
197. *Ibid.*, III. 7.
198. *Ibid.*, II. 1.
199. Kam. I. II.
200. Ap. Dh. S. I. 9.23.6.
201. *Ibid.*, II. 1. 2. 12.
202. Ap. Dh. S., II. 1.2.3. 203. Vas. Dh. S. V. 1.
204. Manu, I. 108.
205. *Ibid.*, II. 5.

duties.[206] Conversely, a vaisya who has fallen off from his duty becomes Maitraksajyotika Preta, who feeds on pus; and a sudra a Cailasaka Preta, who feeds on mouths.[207] The theory of the transmigration of soul makes the benefits of following one's duty still larger, for the benefits are no longer confined to the existing material life but are projected to the life after the present one. Although righteous conduct is productive of beneficial results to the individual in this world, he should also appreciate that wordly benefits are after all produced only as accessories to the fulfilment of law, just as in the case of a mango tree, which is planted in order to obtain fruit, shade and fragrance are accessory advantages.[208]

One should, therefore, fulfil one's sacred duties not merely to acquire objects such as fame, gain and honour but also for the benefit after death.[209]

One of the main objectives of the laws of smrtis appear to inculcate among the men of different castes the spirit and conviction to follow gladly and without any grudge the duties laid down for their caste. In a society dominated largely by religious and theological concepts, the daily material life and work could be influenced much more by religious, theological and superstitious precepts and teachings than we can think of in later times when scence and civilization undermine considerably such ideas and precepts. The smrtis seem to rely on teachings based on religion, and such idealist philosophies as the transmigration of soul, etc. which seek to establish the much needed conviction among the members of the different classes and castes, including the lowest amongst them, that it lay in their own interest, both in this life and in the much more important life afterwards, to practise zealously the duties laid down for them by the dharma laws. Thus one of the methods adopted by the smrtis for the preservation and perpetuation of the class exploitation

206. Ap. Dh. S. II. 5.11.10.
207. Manu, XII. 72.
208. Ap. Dh. S. 1. 7.20.3.
209. *Ibid.*, 1.7.20.1.

of the social and economic system of the period was to lay a theoretical basis for eulogising and idealising that system and convince even the downtrodden sections of its utility.

The smrtis are at the same time aware that under the changed circumstances it is no longer possible or desirable to in one's hope in the dutiful performance of dharma. It might be true of earlier times when life was not much complicated and society was not constituted of mutually hostile economic classes. Naturally men are no longer virtuous now as in the days of the golden past. Narada has said likewise also Brhaspati.[210] Brhaspati laments that in former ages men were strictly virtuous and devoid of mischievous: propensities whereas now avarice and malice have taken, possession of men, thus necessitating the use of judicial proceedings. Transgression of law and violence are noticed even among great men in the past, and such lapses may be treated as precedents in the later ages. Gautama, therefore, asserts that they have no force as precedents to guide the conduct of men in later ages.[211] Lawgivers are also conscious of the existence in society of "despicable systems of philosophy" which are not based on the Vedas. Manu declares that such philosophies do not produce any award after death as they are founded on darkness.[212] The Veda is asserted with vehemence to be the eternal eye of the manes, gods and men.[213] All such doctrines as differ from. the Veda spring us and soon perish, are worthless and false, because they are of later origin.[214] It appears that the theoretical edifice of the Veda philosophy was being: challenged by the formidable philosophy of the Lokayatikas. Vatsayayana furnishes an example of this ideological challenge posed by the Lokayatikas who consider the observance of religious practices useless. because their results, if any, appear only in the next life, which is doubtful. Thus the growing antagonism

207. Manu, XII. 72.
208. Ap. Dh. S. 1.7.20.3.
209. *Ibid.*, 1.7.20.1.
210. Nar., Int. 1.1-2.
211. Gaut. Dh. S. 1.3.
212. Manu, XII. 95.

and the challenge to the very basic tenets and philosophy of the Vedas and tradition offered by the materialistic philosophy of the Lokayatikas made it necessary for the smrtis to lay down laws which were to be enforced by the king and the state for the preservation of the social order. The need for the application of danda grew, and emphasis was laid down on a sound dandaniti (punishment) which alone, as the Arthasastra of Kautilya puts it, can procure the safety and security of life.[215] Danda is represented as "a means to make acquisitions, to keep them secure, to improve them, and to distribute among the deserved the profit of improvement."[216] When the law of punishment is kept in abeyance, it gives rise to such disorder as prevails in the world of fishes; for in the absence of a magistrate (dandadhara bhave), the strong will swallow the weak; but under his protection the weak will resist the strong.[217]

"Thus people (Loka), consisting of four castes and four orders of religious life, when governed by the king with his sceptre, will keep to their respective paths, ever devotedly adhering to their respective duties and occupations."[218]

The smrti laws borrow heavily from the Arthasastra of Kautilya the necessity and desirability of using punishment (danda) as a means to keep the various castes in check and to compel them to perform their duties in accordance with the rules. The king is to keep in secret confinement a person who violates the rules of his caste or order and if he does not amend he is to be banished.[219] The king should pay attention to the laws of countries, the sub-divisions of castes and families, and make the four castes (varna) fulfil their respective duties.[220] The duty of the king is to keep the four

213. *Ibid.*, XII. 94.
214. *Ibid.*, XII. 96.
215. Kam., I. II. 25-30.
216. AS., BK. I. Ch. V.
217. *Ibid.*, BK. I. Ch. V.
218. *Ibid.*, BK. I. Ch. V.
219. *Ibid.*, BK. I. Ch. V.
220. Ap. Dh. S. II. 10.27. 18-19.

castes and four orders in the practice of their several duties.[221] He should punish those who stray from the path of duty.[222] The king should carefully compel the vaisyas and sudras to perform the work prescribed for them; for if these two castes swerved from their duties, they would throw this whole world into confusion.[223] A man of low castes, who through covetousness lives by the occupations of a higher one, should be deprived of his property and banished by the king.[224] Yajnavalkya ordains that families, castes, srenis, ganas and janapadas, which have deviated from their duties, should be disciplined and set on the right path.[225] If they did not inflict punishment on those worthy to be punished, the stronger would roast the weaker, like a fish on a spit.[226] Ownership would not remain with anyone, and the lower ones would usurp the place of the higher ones.[227] Manu bluntly states the role of punishment thus:

"The whole world is kept in order by punishment for a guiltless man is hard to find; through fear of punishment the whole world yields the enjoyments (which it owes)."[228]

According to Narada if the king does not inflict punishment which is his duty, the vaisyas will abandon their work and the sudras eclipse all the rest.[229] When any caste lags behind the rest or outsteps the limits assigned to it, the king must bring it back to the path of the duty.[230]

If he fails in doing this then created beings of this world shall perish.[231]

---

221. Ap. Dh. S. XIX. 7.
222. Visnu, III. 3.
223. Vas. Dh. S. XIX. 8; Visnu, III. 37.
224. Manu, VIII. 418.
225. *Ibid.*, X. 96.
226. Yaj. 1.361.
227. Manu, VII. 20.
228. *Ibid.*, VI1. 21.
229. *Ibid.*, VII. 22.
230. Nar., XVIII. 16.
231. *Ibid.*, XVIII. 16; Yaj. 1.360.

Chapter

11

Laws on Family

The smrti portions of the epic devoted to related topics; and the puranas give considerable attention to different aspects of family, especially on marriage. There is a clear recognition in the Santi Parva that the form and content of marriage prevailing during the early centuries of the Christian era, were not eternal but had emerged out of sex relations which were quite at variance with them. Bhisma characterises the sex relations of the four yugas by four names namely samkalpa in the krta yuga, sams parsa in the treta, maithuna in dvapara and dvandva in the kali.[1] Samkalpa relations have been identified as those of complete promiscuity, samsparsa as those in which relations between the nearest relatives were banned and marriage between members of the same gotra were forbidden. The maithuna form of marriage marks the end of group marriage and in it the pairing family endures till the pair desires to the exclusion of others. Dvandva is the monogamous pair of the kali age in which woman is subjected to man.[2] The early Vedic society was overwhelmingly tribal and communal, and

1. SP., 207. 38-41.
2. S.A. Dange, India from Primitive Communism to Slavery, pp. 67-68.

we do not have clear and direct proof of strictly monogamous patriarchal family; and the other hand the terms jana and vis are mentioned there about 275 and on 271 times respectively.[3]

The Santi Parva clearly shows the prevalence of a monogamous family. It states: "A householder's home even if filled with sons, daughters-in-law and servants, is regard empty if destitute of the housewife. One's house is not one's home; only one's wife is one's home."[4] Pativrata wife's attention to the wishes and needs of the husband, receives much praise in this tract. Such a wife is the chief helper of the husband in the pursuit of dharma, artha and kama. She is the prime wealth of man, and even those who are otherwise helpless derive help from such a wife.[5] Such an ideal wife should know that even gods are pleased only when the husband is satisfied.[6] The husband with whom marriage is solemnised is not merely a husband but he is the prime god to his wife. The wife of a dissatisfied husband is reduced to ashes.[7] These glimpses of relations between husband and wife are contained in the story of a pigeon and its spouse. It is, however, obvious that the description given here must reflect the ruling ideas and concepts relating to the relationshp between husband and wife in the contemporary form of monogamous marriages.

Although in the type of the monogamous family depicted there appears to be much feelings of comradeship, love and respect of the husband for his wife, yet it is evident that the position of the wife is decidedly unequal and inferior to that of the husband who has already assumed the role of a lord. The wife can think of her salvation only by keeping her lord satisfied through her services. We do not have sufficient materials at hand to enable us to say definitely about the existence, nature and form of mother right in remote history. During our period, however, it is father right

3. R.S. Sharma, Aspects of Political Ideas and Institutions in Ancient India, p. 80.
4. SP., 144.56.
5. *Ibid.*, 144.10.14.
6. *Ibid.*, 145.3.
7. *Ibid.*, 145.42.

and the supremacy of man over woman that rules. The form and essence of marriage in vogue represent the subjugation of women to men who had all superior rights. The various forms of marriage prevalent and recognised as lawful underline the fact that woman had lost the battle to man.

Kautilya and the smrti-kars describe the various forms of marriages. There are eight forms of marriages according to the Arthasastra. One of them, the brahma marriage is one in which a well adorned maiden is given in marriage to the bridegrooms.[8] Gautama describes the ideal bridegroom to be a person possessing sacred learning, virtuous conduct, a good disposition and having relatives.[9] A prajapatya marriage is intended for the joint performance of the sacred duties by a man and a woman.[10] The formula is "fulfil ye the law conjointly."[11] When the bridegroom presents a cow and a bull to the person having authority over the maiden it is said to be the arsa form of marriage.[12] Narada includes dress also among the presents.[13]

In the daiva marriage a bride is given to an officiating priest in a sacrifice.[14] The gandharva marriage takes place as a result of the voluntary union of a bride with her lover.[15] This is spontaneous union with a willing maiden.[16] The girl and the lover unite themselves through love.[17] Vasistha limits it to lovers of equal caste.[18] While Manu describes it to be the voluntary union of a maiden and a lover and says that it

8. AS., BK. III, Ch. n.
9. Gaut. Dh. S., IV. 6; Ap. Dh. S., 11.5.11-17; Baud. Dh.S., 1. 11.20.2; Nar., XII. 40.
10. AS., BK. III. Ch. II.
11. Gaut. Dh. S., IV. 15; Baud. Dh. S., 1.11.20.3; Nar., XII. Yaj., I. 60; Manu, III. 30.
12. Gaut. Dh. S., IV. 15; Ap. Dh. S., 2.5.
13. Nar., XII. 41.
14. AS., BK. III. Ch. II; Gaut. Dh. S., IV. 9; Manu, III. 28; Vas. J. Dh. S., I. 31; Baud. Dh. S., 1. 11.20.5.
15. AS., BK. III. Ch. n.
16. Gmt. Dh. S., IV. 10; Nar., XII. 42; Baud. Dh. S., 1. 11.20.6.
17. Ap. Dh. S., n. 5.11.20.
18. Vas. Dh. S., 1. 33.

"springs from desire and has sexual intercourse for its purpose."[19] In the asura form a maiden is given in marriage after receiving plenty of wealth (sulka).[20] Here persons having authority over the maiden are "propitiated by money."[21] Vasistha calls it a manusa tight where, after making a bargain with the father, the suitor marries a damsel purchased on payment of money.[22] According to Manu if the bridegroom receives a maiden after having given as much wealth as he can afford, to the kinsmen and to the bride herself, it is called asura marriage.[23] A raksasa marriage is based on the abduction of the maiden[24] as the bridegroom and his friends take away the bride,[25] after having overcome her father or relations by force.[26] Vasistha calls such a forcible abduction of a damsel after destroying her relatives by strength of arms a marriage by ksatra right. Manu gives a more vivid picture of such a forcible abduction of maiden from her home while she cries out and weeps, after (her kinsmen) have been slain or wounded and their houses broken open."[27] The paisaca marriage is also based on abduction of a maiden while she is asleep and in a state of intoxication.[28] According to Baudhayana it takes place with a maiden who is sleeping, intoxicated or out of her senses with fear or passion.[29] Narada calls it the basest of all the marriages.[30]

Thus, as many as eight forms of marriage were in vogue during that period. The difference in the essential content of the different kinds of marriages is so great that neither the society at large nor the lawgivers of the time

19. Manu, III. 32.
20. Vas. Dh. S., I. 33.
21. Gaut. Dh. S., IV. 11; Ap. Dh. S., II. 5.12.1; Baud. Dh. S. I. 11.20.7.
22. Vas. Dh. S., I. 35.
23. Manu, III. 31.
24. AS., Bk. III. Ch. II; Baud. Dh. S., I.11.20.8.
25. Ap. Dh. S., II. 5.12.2; Gaut. Dh. S., IV. 12.
26. Vas. Dh. S., I. 34.
27. Manu, III. 33.
28. AS., Bk. III. Ch. II. 174; Gaut. Dh. S., IV. 14.
29. Baud. Dh. S., 1.11.20.9; Manu, III. 34.
30. Nar., XII. 43.

could view all the forms of marriages with equai esteem. The smrti-kars naturally give different appraisals of different forms of marriages. All marriages are not recognised as 1awful. Gautama recognises as lawful only the first four ends of marriages, i.e. brahma, prajapatya, arsa and daiva.[31] Baudhayana considers the first four forms of marriages as lawful for a brahmana.[32] Among these also each preceding form is preferable to the succeeding one. Apastamba considers only brahma, arsa and daiva forms as praiseworthy, each preceding one being better than the one following. Manu makes the legality or otherwise of these marriages dependent upon the varna.[33] For brahmanas the first six forms of marriages are declared to be lawful whereas for ksatriyas it is the last four ones. A vaisya and a sudra have only asura and gandharva forms available.[34] He firmly lays down that the paisaca and asura rites must never be used.[35]

For ksatriya, gandharva and raksasa, whether separate or mixed, are permitted by the sacred tradition.[36] Lawgivers provide a yardstick by which the quality of a particular form of marriage is evaluated. The form of marriage is linked with the quality of the progeny. The quality of the offspring is dependent upon the quality of the marriage rite.[37] Manu elaborates this cause and effect theory in greater detail. The son of a wife wedded according to the brahma rite if he performs meritorious acts liberates from sixteen ancestors, ten descendents and himself as the twenty-first.[38] The number of ancestors and descendents goes on decreasing according to the declining quality of the marriage rite.[39] Manu in effect condemns the remaining four forms of marriage including the gandharva form as "blamable marriages" giving birth to sons

31. Gaut. Dh. S., IV. 14.
32. Ap. Dh. S., II. 5.12.3.
33. Manu, III. 22.
34. *Ibid.*, III. 23.
35. *Ibid.*, III. 25.
36. Manu, III. 26.
37. Ap. Dh. S., II. 5.12.4.
38. Manu, III. 37.
39. *Ibid.*, III. 38.

who are cruel and speakers of untruth, and who hate the Veda and the sacred law. "In the blameless marriages blameless children are born to men, in blamable (marriages) blamable (off-spring); one should therefore avoid the blamable (forms of marriage)."[40] The provision of the four approved forms of marriage is meant generally for the members of the two privileged and royal varnas, i.e. the brahmanas and ksatriyas is considered by Dr. Sharma as significant from another point of view. The fact that these forms of marriage are confined to only dharma[41] signifies that the patriarchal element is supreme in them and not in the unapproved forms of marriage where the sanction was required not only of the father but also of the mother.[42] It appears that .among the royal and privileged varnas of ksatriyas the supremacy of father-right over mother-right was fully tablished and .consolidated as a result of which the question of the consent of the mother in marriage was ruled out. On the contrary in the cases of the other varnas it was still relevant as their womenfolk still retained considerable independence on account of their participation in productive processes. Since the brahmanas and ksatriyas were responsible for upholding the social order of the day, it was natural for the lawgivers to prescribe and insist that they conform to the ideal forms of marriage.

Whatever may be the principles or criteria laid down by the lawgivers for praising or condemning a particular form of marriage the irresistible conclusion emerges that excepting the gandharva form of marriage in no other form there was either the choice or love and affection of women at any consequence. She was given in marriage in utter disregard of her choice in the brahma, asura, daiva, prajapatya forms of marriages though these have been so much praised and declared to be virtuous by the smrti-kars. She is a victim of brutal force in raksasa marriage, and the

40. *Ibid.*, III. 41-42.
41. Gaut. Dh. S., IV. 14-15; Visnu, XIV. 27-28; Nar., XII. 44; AS. III. Ch. II.
42. R.S. Sharma, Light on Early Indian Society and Economy, p. 42.

paisaca marriage is nothing but an ordeal and bestial torture imposed on her. The asura marriage is based not only on a complete absence of the desire or consent of the maiden to the marriage, but it also underlines the degraded position to which women had been subjected to. She is now sold and purchased like a commodity or any property. While the other forms of marriages are no exceptions, the asura form of marriage appears to be the crudest expression of the invasion of the institution of private property into the realm of family and marriage. Here woman is as good or as bad as any other property. She can be alienated to anyone like a saleable commodity or property. Vasistha not only states that the damsel is purchased for money but quotes in support the following from the Veda:

"Therefore one hundred (cows) besides a chariot should be given to the father of the bride."[43] Apastamba too refers; to the Veda prescribing the same price. Fulfilment of law demands that at the time of marriage a gift should be made by the bridegroom to the father of the bride. Apastamba almost blushes at the involvement of the element of sale in marriage and tries to explain it away as "a metaphorical expression."[44]

That the dominant view of the society as well as the declared objective of the privileged classes and the law-givers was to deprive women of all independence and free choice in matters of marriage and family is evident from the open hostility and contempt with which the smrti law-givers look at the gandharva form of marriage, the only form based on love and willingness of women. As we have already seen, Manu refers to this form of marriage in a deriding tone. It is true that recognition is extended to this form of marriage grudgingly but its legality is restricted only to the vaisyas and sudras, but these two castes are described with contempt as not being particular about their wives and subsisting by such low occupations as husbandry and service.[45] However Baudhayana recommends gandharva marriage for all castes

---

43. Vas. Dh. S., I. 35-36.
44. Ap. Dh. S., II. 6.14.12.

on the ground that it is based on mutual love.[46] Vatsyayana also states that according to some sages prosperity always results from marrying the girl to whom one becomes attached, and that therefore no other girl should be married by anyone.[47] This opinion favouring the marriage based on mutual love appears to be at best a feeble voice of a dissenting minority which must have been drowned by the trumpeting chorus of the authoritative lawgivers idealising, in the name of virtuous offsprings of the craze of the age—the first four forms of marriages, all of which are conspicuous by the absence of any voice or say of the maiden in her marriage.

Another important problem before the smrti-kars appears to be that of the children. The growth of property and the desire for its transmission to children was in reality the moving power which brought in monogamy to ensure legitimate heirs and to limit their number to the actual progeny of the married pair.[48] The growth of property appears to have invariably acted as a strong motive force for men to ensure the legitimacy of their children, especially the sons who would inherit the property. The Aryan society is also not an exception to this and this problem received attention of the smrti-kars in considerable measure. In this respect the Aryan women's condition was very much similar to the condition of Greek women. The Greek concept of family during the historical period resembles the family evolved by our smrti-kars. In Greece, the object of having a family was two-fold. First, the declaration that the chief object of marriage was the procreation of children in lawful wedlock; and second, the seclusion of women to ensure the result.[49]

The seriousness of the confusion regarding the different origins of sons can be realised from the fact that we get an

45. Baud. Dh. S., 1.11.20. 13-15.
46. Baud. Dh. S., I. 11. 20. 16.
47. Kam., III. 1. 14-15.
48. Lewis Henry Morgan, Ancient Society, p. 485.
49. *Ibid.*, p. 484.

impressive list of different kinds of sons owing their birth to different circumstances and fathers, often outside the strictly monogamous pair. We find the mention of a legitimate son, a son begotten on the wife by a kinsman, an adopted son, a son made, a son born secretly and a son abandoned by his natural parents.[50] Besides there are sons of an unmarried girl, the son of a pregnant bride, the son of a twice married woman, the son of an appointed daughter, a son self given and a son bought.[51] Manusmrti too mentions different kinds of sons[52] and introduces the distinction that certain kinds of sons are only kinsmen whereas others are both kinsmen and heirs.[53]

It is worthwhile to see in detail the problem of the sons begotten outside wedlock and the confusion regarding the ownerships of stich sons. Gautama permits a woman whose husband is dead to bear a son to her brother-in-law.[54] On failure of a brother-in-law she may obtain offspring by cohabiting with a sapinda, a sagotra, a samanapravara or on who belongs to the same caste.[55] He adds:

> "The child belongs to him who beget it, except if an agreement (to the contrary has been made). (And the child begotten at) a living husband's (request) on his wife (belongs to the husband), (But if it was begotten) by a stranger (it belongs) to the latter, or to both (the natural father and the husband of the mother). But being reared by the husband, (it belongs to him)."[56]

The above rules indicate the undisguised views of the lawgivers that the feelings of love or chastity of a wife were matter of no consequence. The only important consideration

---

50. Gaut. Dh. S., XXVIII. 32.
51. *Ibid.*, XXVIII. 33.
52. Manu, IX. 31-56.
53. *Ibid.*, IX. 160; Yaj., II. 128-132; Baud. Dh. S., II.
54. Gaut. Dh. S., XVIII. 4.
55. *Ibid.*, XVIII. 6.
56. Gaut. Dh. S., XVIII. 9-10, 12-14.

was that the property-owning man should have a son who inherit, even if it involves lending of his wife to someone else for producing an heir.[57]

The rules quoted above further show that begetting a son, and claiming ownership is a matter of agreement in which the husband invites another man to beget child on his wife and the husband owns the child. According to Baudhayana the son begotten by another, on the wife of a deceased man, Of a eunuch, or of one incurably deceased, after permission is given, is called a ksetraja son.[58] With such types of sons we may safely presume that these sons, more often than not, may have been a source of various claims and counter-claims on the properties and inheritance, and consequently also a cause of much stress and strain on the family and society. Their claims to inheritance could not be ruled out easily; in fact the lawgivers are on record to extend to ksetraja sons a considerable degree of recognition and rights. Such a son begotten on a wife has two fathers and belongs to two families; he has a right to perform the funeral oblations and to inherit the property of his two fathers.[59] The issues of these women who are purchased for price belong to the begetter. But when nothing has been paid by such a purchaser-begetter, the offspring belongs to the legitimate husband of the woman.[60] The smrti-kars emphasise again and again the role of women as a means of production of children. The production of children, the nurture of these and the daily life of men, (of these matters) woman is visibly the cause.[61] Women have been created for the sake of procreation.[62] There appears to be a craze for having male issues, who were perhaps considered important not only on account of their usefulness in the process of production and acquisition of wealth but also for inheriting the properties as

57. Gaut. Dh. S., XVIII. 12.
58. Baud. Dh. S., II. 2. 3. 17; Manu, IX.
59. Baud. Dh. S., II. 2. 3. 17.
60. Nar., XII. 54.
61. Manu, IX. 27.
62. Nar. XII. 19.

natural heirs in a society dominated by the property-owning classes. Besides, the male issues not only fulfilled the pious longing of the father but also gave him the additional satisfaction of continuing his lineage. According to Apastamba the Vedas declare, "In thy offspring thou art born again, that, mortal, is thy immortality." Or these sons who live fufilling the rites taught in the Veda increase the fame and heavenly bliss of their departed ancestors.[64] The father passes his debt on to the son and obtains immortality if he sees the face of a living son.[65] Through the sons he conquers the world and through a grandson he obtains immortality, but through his sons grandson he gains the world of the sun.[66] The son presents the funeral oblations to his father even though he inherits no property. He has the quality of saving his father from the hell called put and therefore, a male child is called putra (protector from putra).[67] Endless are the word's of those who have sons; there is no place for the man who is destitute of the male offspring.[68] The smrtis are unanimous about the unique role of son, but they are faced with the problem of ensuring the legitimacy of sons and ensuring their ownership strictly to the father in the family.

The primary objective of the smrti laws, therefore, now appears to be the establishment of complete monogamy for the Aryan woman and ensure that those sons begotten by the husband alone are only genuine. Different kinds of sons naturally give rise to disputes regarding their ownership. The only undisputed matter in this confusion and conflict of claims is that the son nowhere belongs to the mother, the woman who bears him. This fully underlines the complete defeat of mother-right in a sphere where mother's role was so important.

The smrti-kars are concerned here with entirely different problem, namely, who of the two persons, the

63. Ap. Dh. S., II. 9.24.1.
64. *Ibid.*, II. 9.24.3.
65. Vas. Dh. S., XVII. 1; Manu, IX.107.
66. *Ibid.*, XVII. 5; Manu, IX. 137.
67. Visnu, XV. 43-44; Br., XXV. 36.
68. Vas. Dh. S.. XVII. 2.

husband of the wife or the begetter of the child shall have the rightful claim over the son. This conflict persists probably on account of the fact that promiscuous intercourse is still prevalent on a large scale, and the institution of mono gamous marriage is not so well established as to eliminate large-scale promiscuous intercourse and adultery. This has serious implications for the class-ridden society and the property-owning classes. The lawgivers have to find out a satisfactory solution which could set at rest the recurring controversy around the ownership of the sons, the heirs ot the property owners.

They have two solutions. First, they declare that woman is also a property and a means of production in the same way as the other properties such as land or cattle. This is evident from the way they liken women to a field or soil or even to a female camel, etc.

Civil laws applicable to property relations are applied to women who are now transformed into property by these philosopher jurists. Denying the claim of the male begetter to the offspring against the husband. Manu decides the matter on the basis of the property relationship regarding cattle wealth. He says that in the case of cows, mares, female camels, slave girls, buffalo cows, she goats and ewe it is not the begetter (or his owner) who obtain the offspring.[69] According to Narada when the seed is sown in the field of another with the consent of the owner of the field the offspring is considered to be the common property of the giver of the seed and the owner of the soil.[70] Therefore, according to Manu, "men who have no marital property in women, but sow their seed in the soil of others benefit the owner of the women; but the giver of the seed reaps no advantage."[71] In this way the controversy regarding claim over progeny is sought to be settled through the accepted precepts and laws relating to the private property belonging to the privileged classes. The smrti-kars evidently have

69. Manu, IX. 48, 49.
70. Nar., XII. 5-8; Manu, IX. 53.
71. Manu, IX. 51.

treated the woman (wife) as an item of property while seeking to settle the claim over progeny.

Another method to safeguard the legitimacy of the progeny was to deprive the woman of all independence and to keep her in complete subjugation. The only means for her to obtain bliss in heaven is to show obedience to her husband.[72] To remain subject in her infancy to her father, in her youth to her husband, and in her old age to her sons, is the fate allotted to her by the smrti lawgivers.[73] The peculiar contrivance of archaic jurisprudence for retaining Aryan women in the bondage of the family for life is very much similar in principle to the institutions of perpetual tutelage in the oldest Roman law, whereby a female, though relieved from her parents' authority by his decease, continues to be subject to her nearest male relations; or to her father's nominees, as her guardian.[74] A wife is not independent with respect to the fulfilment of the sacred law.[75] 'There is complete unanimity among the smrti-kars that woman has to be kept under subjugation by men from her radle to the grave and she should not be allowed any independence whatsoever.

Having based the legal ownership of son on the principles of private property, the smrti-kars prescribe the subjugation of women through various forms as a means to safeguard the purity of children and family. A comprehensive philosophical edifice is created to achieve this objective. It is propounded that women are born to be kept under man's protection and subjugation throughout her life, that is from her cradle to her death women do not possess independence. "Their father protects (them) in childhood, their husband protects (them) in youth, and their sons protect (them) in old age; a woman is never fit for independence."[76] Gautama does not consider a wife independent with respect to the fulfilment

---

72. Visnu, XXV. 3.
73. Manu, IX. 3; Visnu, XXV. 13; Nar., XIII. Baud. Dh. S., II. 2.3.44; Vas. Dh. S., V. 2.
74. H.S. Maine, Ancient Law, p. 153.
75. Gaut. Dh. S., XVIII. 1.

of the sacred law. She is thought to be destitute of strength.[77] The sole purpose of her existence is to be useful to the husband, and as such she is ordained not even to decorate herself with ornaments nor to participate in amusements while her husband is away from home.[78] According to Narada: Independence to woman is harmful. It is through independence that women go to ruin though born in a noble family.[79]

A creature has to be evil and vile to deserve its loss of independence. Woman is certainly one in the view of the smrti-kars. No reliance can be placed on a woman for want of veracity in her, and as such she is ineligible to become a witness.[80] Manu finds in woman a passion for man, irritable temper and natural heartlessness on account of which they become disloyal towards their husbands.[81] The evil character of woman dates back to the time of creation itself when Manu attributed to women a love of their bed, of their seat and of ornament, impure desires, wrath, dishonesty, malice and bad conduct.[82] They are so lowly in moral standards that they do not even care for beauty, nor take into account the age of a man but give themselves as readily to the handsome as to the ugly "thinking, (it is enough that) he is a man."[83] She is painted as a seducer of men in this world and I considered so dangerous a creature that even a learned man may be borne a slave of desire and anger in the face of her seduction.

If woman is such a vile creature she must naturally be guarded suitably by men. Guarding of woman is considered by Manu the highest duty of all castes, and even weak

76. Jcaud. Dh. S. II. 2.3.44-45; Manu, IX. 3; Yaj., I. 85; Vas. Dh. S.,. V. 2; Visnu, XXV. 13; Nar., XIII. 31.
77. Gaut. Dh. S., XVIII. 1.
78. Visnu, XXV. 9.
79. Nar., XIII. 30.
80. *Ibid.*, XV. 191; Yaj., n. 70; Visnu, VII. 1. 10.
81. Manu, IX.15.
82. *Ibid.*, IX.17.
83. *Ibid.*, IX.14.

husbands must strive to guard their wives.[84] She must be kept independence day and night by the male members of the families and if they attach themselves to several enjoyments they must be kept under one's control.[85] They should not resort to the houses of strangers.[86] They are forbidden to stand near the doorway or the window of their houses.[87]

Thus a woman is transformed by man into a captive who has to be kept confined within the house and placed under constant surveillance of the male members. This is the direction contained in the smrtis as we have seen. But is it an easy task for man to guard these human chattel effectively? All lawgivers are conscious of this problem. Manu frankly admits the impossibility of guarding women by force and suggests a device to achieve this objective. The husband should employ his wife in the collection and expenditure of his wealth, in keeping everything clean, in the fulfilment of religious duties, in the preparation of his food and in looking after the household utensils.[88] Brhaspati also prescribes the above expedient.[89] According to Visnu the wife should show reverence to her mother-in-law, father-in-law, gurus, to divinities and to guests by paying attention to them.[90] She should keep household articles, such as the winnowing baskets and the rest in good condition.[91] It is also her duty to be careful about her pestle and mortar and other domestic utensils.[92] It appears that the smrti-writers were guided by the saying that an empty mind is devil's workshop, and the rules laid down above appear to have the objective of keeping the woman constantly employed and burdened with all the

---

84. Manu, IX.6; Yaj., 1.78.
85. Manu, IX.2.
86. Visnu, XXV.10.
87. *Ibid.*, XXV.11.
88. Manu, IX.1O-11.
89. Br., XXIV.4.
90. Visnu, XXV.3.
91. Visnu, XXV.4.
92. *Ibid.*, XXV.6.

domestic labour. In this way the wife is reduced to a domestic slave who has to be constantly kept saddled with work so that she does not find any time or occasion to put in effect the evil design that a vile creature like her is capable of.

The period during which the more important smrtis were compiled saw great economic and cultural progress. Indians and Greeks both contributed to the advancement of mankind as a whole. But the treatment meted out to woman in both these countries is hardly complimentary. Morgan considers it an enigma that a race (Greek), with endowments great enough to impress their mental life upon the world, should have remained essentially barbaric in their treatment of the female sex at the height of their civilization.[93] The remark is fully applicable to our own country during the period under consideration.

Our study and appraisal of the position of women in the smrtis will be incomplete, in fact, incorrect, if we lose sight of those provisions which tend to mitigate the harshnesses towards women limited though they may be. On the one hand certain rules in the smrtis seek the prevention of cruelty to women while on the other, other rules advocate extending courtesy within the range of privileges allowed them. We have already examined the views of Manu on many fundamental aspects concerning women, but he also states that women must be honoured and adored by their fathers, brothers, husbands and brothers-in-law who desire their own welfare.[94] Manu feels that honouring and adoring women are conducive to the happiness and prosperity of the family and *vice-versa*.[95] Yajnavalkya holds the same opinion on this matter, and its purpose according to the Mitaksara is that when women are respected they increase dharma (piety), artha (wealth) and kama (pleasure).[96] Apastamba lays down that a son must constantly serve his mother, even though she

93. Lewis Henry Morgan, Ancient Society, p. 242.
94. Manu, III.55.
95. *Ibid.*, III. 56-57.
96. Yaj., I. 82.

be fallen, for a mother does many acts for her son.[97] The Arthasastra of Kautilya positively forbids abusing of wives by the husband as also beating her either with a bamboo bark or with rope, or with palm.[98] Vasistha advocates tolerance on the part of the husband even when the wife is tainted with sin or is quarrelsome or has left the house or has suffered from criminal assault, she must not be abandoned as sacred law does not prescribe forsaking lier.[99] He is for reproving a wife, sons and pupils defiled by sinful deeds. It is only when they do not amend themselves that they should be cast off.[100] Apastamba lays down that the husband, if he forsakes his wife unjustly, should be made to put on apes skin and should be made to beg in several houses saying: "Give alms to him who forsook his wife."[101]

Yajnavalkya states that the person who abandons an obedient, skilful and pleasant speaking wife should be made to give one-third of his property to her.[102] It also provides for remarriage of women under certain circumstances such as having waited sufficiently for the return of the husband who has gone abroad.[103]

It is difficult to assess the efficacy of the rules of the smrtis in ameliorating the condition of women. The bask attitude of the smrtis being so hostile to women regarding their acumen, character, and the very purpose of birth, it is difficult to believe that these rules had any substantial bearing in making their lot better.

The institution of marriage as enunciated, is monogamous only for the woman (and sudras) but not for the twice-born men who are allowed by the smrti laws to marry more than one wife. Apastamba restricts men from taking a second wife only so long as the present wife is

---

97. Ap. Dh. S., 1.10-28.9.
98. AS., BK. III. Ch. III.
99. Vas. Dh. S., XXVIII. 2-3.
100. *Ibid.*, XIII. 49.
101. Ap. Dh. S., I. 10.28.19.
102. Yaj. I. 76.
103. AS., BK. III. Ch. IV.

willing and able to perform her share of religious duties and bears a son.[104] Baudhayana prescribes proclaiming in the village a wife who, being obdurate against her husband, makes herself sterile, as one who destroys embryos.

Such a wife should be driven out from the house.[105] He permits the abandoning of a barren wife in the tenth year, one who bears daughter only in the twelfth year, and one whose children all died in the fifteenth year. But if the wife is quarrelsome the husband is advised to abandon her without delay.[106] Kautilya allows man to marry any woman because women are created for the sake of sons.[107]

He too prescribes a period of waiting by the husband for the birth of son after which if a son is not born he is permitted to marry another woman.[108] Yajnavalkya allows more than one wife to the brahmana, ksatriya and vaisya.[109]

Before we go into the question of women's share in inheritance it is worthwhile to examine in brief the prohibition of marriage within the gotra. The smrtis forbid the marriage of a woman to a man of the same gotra.[110]

Gautama recommends marriage between persons who have not the same pravaras.[111] Manu recommends a girl who is neither a sapinda nor belongs to the same family on the father side for marriage.[112] According to Narada sagotras and samana pravaras are ineligible for marriage up to the fifth and seventh degrees of relationship respectively on the father's and mother's side.

This restriction on marriage within the gotra (gens) is significant. With a descent in the male line the gotra or the gens embraced all persons who traced their descent from a

104. Ap. Dh. S., II. 5. II. 12.
105. Baud. Dh. S., IV. 1.20.
106. *Ibid.*, II. 2.4.6; Manu, IX. 81.
107. AS., BK. III. Ch. II.
108. *Ibid.*, BK. III. Ch. II.
109. Yaj., II. S. 7.
110. Ap. Dh. S., 11.5.11.15.
111. Gaut. Dh. S., IV.2.
112. Manu, III.5.

common male ancestor. The gotra would include this ancestor and his children, the children of his son and the children of his male descendants, through males, in perpetuity; whilst the children of his daughters and the children of his female descendants, through females, would belong to other gotras namely those of their respective fathers.[113] This shows that the Aryan community had understood the evils of consanguine marriages, and by imposing this restriction they sought to increase the vigour of the stock. The advantages of marriages between unrelated persons through the practice of marrying out of the gens were fully realised.

Tllis principle is of far-reaching consequence for the members of the gens owning property. With the assured paternity of "children it was possible for them to maintain their exclusive right to the property of their deceased father. Under this principle the female children were necessarily to be given in marriage to the male belonging to some other gens. If the right of inheritance could be confined to the male children alone to the exclusion of the female ones, it was possible not only to deny the female sex any right to property of the family and therefore also the gens, but also to prevent the properties of the family and the gens from slipping out of their hands.

The smrtis reiterated the same legal principles as perhaps had already become an accepted usage in society from before. All the smrtis disqualify the daughter from inheriting the property of the deceased father. The son alone has the right of inheritance. As such women have dearly been disenfranchised from the inheritance or property. Man is property owning, woman is property less. According to the Arthasastra of Kautilya if a man has no male issue his own brothers or persons who have been living with him shall take possession of his property.[114] Only in the event of the absence of the persons belonging to these categories a daughter may inherit the property. Manu, however, states that between a son's son and son of a daughter there exists in this world no

113. Lewis Henry Morgan, Ancient Society, p. 67.
114. AS., BK. III. Ch. V.

difference.[115] He also states that between a son's son and the son of an appointed daughter there is no difference either with respect to worldly matters or to sacred duties,[116] According to Jayaswal this was the result of the high regard for the daughter shown by Manu,[117] This rule is, however, capable of a different interpretation. It is not so much the high regard for the daughter as the performance of the funeral rites of a father without a son which explains the rule of Manu. For Manu states that he who has no son may make his daughter an appointed daughter (putrika) saying to the husband: "the (male) child, born of her, shall perform my funeral rites."[118] This rule does not appear .to be an exclusive innovation of Manu. Gautama, who gave his law-book prior to Manu also makes such a provision in the context of inheritance of property. Vasistha also provides for the inheritance of property of a sonless father by the son of an appointed daughter.[119] Therefore if 'We look at this rule of Manu in this context it is evident that Manu has in mind here the son of an appointed-daughter, and he does not render the daughter's appointment as useless as interpreted by Jayaswal'. Thus here too "the daughter is important only because she promises the 'birth of a son for her sonless father'."

Yajnavalkya states that if a person dies without having a son of any of the twelve kinds then wife, daughter, mother, father, brother, brother's son, etc. will inherit the property in the order as stated.[120] It is evident that in the scheme of Yajnavalkya, wife, daughter and mother, though inferior to the twelve kinds of sons, are placed superior to the near relatives of the deceased such as father, brother, as well as bandhus and sagotras. This is certainly an improvement in the position of women heirs: compared to the past. It appears that the smrti-lawyers are in a state of constant conflict with one another as well as with themselves on the question of

115. Manu, Ch. IX. 139.
116. Manu, IX.133.
117. K.P. Jayaswal, Manu and Yajnavalkya, p. 259.
118. Manu, IX.127.
119. Vas. Dh. S., XVII.17.
120. Yaj., II. 135-136.

inheritance by wife or daughters. The conflict of claims is nowhere between the sons and daughters, for against the son or man, the daughters or wife (woman) has lost the battle finally. The conflict appears to be confined only between the daughter and other relations of the sonless deceased?, and his other relatives. An example of such a conflict we find in Brhaspati who states:

> "Although kinsmen (sakulyas), although his father and mother, although uterine brothers be living, the wife of him who dies without leaving male issues shall succeed to his share."[121]

A little further he states:

> "A wife, though preserving her character and though partition have been made, is unworthy to obtain immovable property. Food or a portion of the arable land, shall be given to her at will (for her support)."[122]

Narada states emphatically:

> "On failure of a son, the daughter (succeeds): because she continues the lineage just like (a son); both a son and a daughter continue the lineage of their father."[123]

Further "on failure of daughters, the Sakulyas (are to succeed) and (after them) the Bandhavas; next to member of the same caste. In default of all, that (wealth) goes to the king."[124]

It is evident from the rules quoted above that while Brhaspati is in two minds, he and Narada are also contradicting each other. It is also evident that now the battle-royal for preference in inheritance is going on between

---

121. Br., XXV.48.
122. *Ibid.*, XXV.54.
123. Nar., XIII.50.
124. *Ibid.*, XIII.51.

the daughter (and wife and mother) on the one hand and the Bandhavas, sakulyas and the close male relations of the deceased on the other.

The explanation of the gradual preference accorded to women (daughter, wife and mother, etc.) in inheriting the properties and the exclusion from the same of near male relatives, such as sakulyas, bandhavas etc., appears to lie in a process of the general weakening of the gentile organisation with the right of private property getting established in society. After the rise of private property the undermining of the Aryan gentile organisation, like those of other primitive communities, was inevitable. This process naturally led to a situation in which the individuality of persons began to rise above the gens, or the individuality which so far had been an integral and unidentifiable part of the gens life now craved for itself an independent existence and wider field of operation. The result was the establishment in Aryan society of patriarchal type of family. In the Aryan patriarchal family the heads of the families exercised overriding power over the other family members, male and female. The wife, sons and slaves are dependent, and the head of the family to whom property descends by right of inheritance is independent with regard to all the for:mer.[125] All these persons, i.e. heads of the families, are independent at all times and in relation to those who depend upon them. They can exercise coercion, and the dependents cannot relinquish property without permission of the head of the family.[126] If the son transacts any business without authorisation from father it is declared to be invalid.[127]

When the father distributes his property amongst his sons that is lawful distribution for them and cannot be annulled even if the share of one be less or greater than or equal to the shares of the rest; for (the father is the lord of all).

125. Nar., Y. 34.
126. *Ibid.*, I. 38.
127. *Ibid.*, Y. 30.

According to Vasistha the father has the power to give, to sell and to abandon the son.[128] According to Manu a wife, a son, a slave, these three are declared to have no property; the wealth which they earn is (acquired) for him to whom they belong.[129] These rules clearly indicate the emergence of a family partaking in the nature of a patriarchal institution. It appears that after the patriarchal family undermined the gens it was itself undermined by the same process, i.e. growth of individuality which created it. As the sense of individuality grew along with the growth of private property, the individual members first asserted and then established their own individual property rights, which fact is evident from the recognition of the right of sons to partition by smrtis. As this process continued the positions of the father went down in relation to the near and dear relations of the son who had become a fulfledged owner of his properties by now. His wife, daughter and mother were most directly and intimately connected with him either by blood or by marriage and association. It appears only natural and inevitable that these female relations should have a preference over the other male members of the families, sakulyas, etc. within the framework of the general dominance of father-right over mother-right.[130]

Another important aspect of woman *vis-a-vis* property transactions is unanimous disqualification by the smrtis in entering into transactions relating to property or money. Transactions made by a woman have no validity, especially the gift, hypothecation or sale of house or field, unless of these are sanctioned by the husband or on his failure by the son. They are adjudged to be so, incapable of entering into transactions that Kautilya forbids a wife who has not heard of a debt from being caught hold of for the debt contracted by her husband.[131] According to Narada a wife must not pay a dept contracted by her husband, nor one contracted by her son except if it had been promised by her or contracted by

---

128. Vas. Dh. S., XIV.2; Baud. Dh. S., VII.5.3.
129. Manu, VIII.416.
130. AS., BK. III, Ch. XI.
131. Nar., 1.16.

her in common with her husband. Narada declares that a debt contracted by the wife shall never bind the husband unless it had been contracted at a time when the husband was in distress.[132] Katyayana ordains that a moneylender should never hand over a loan to a dependent woman, to slaves and to minors. The lender cannot recover that which he gives to such persons.[133]

The exemption of woman from the liability of debts may appear to be in favour of woman in so far as it exempts her from the civil action. If, however, we go into the deeper aspect of this question it will become obvious that this protection to woman does not arise from her strength, but is a manifestation of hey, inherent weaknesses in law in matters of property. Narada provides an explanation for woman's position in this matter. He states that a debt must be paid by him who inherits the estate "For the liability for the debts goes together with the right of succession."[134]

That the socalled protection to woman reflects her weakness is also evident from the liability of certain other classes of women in debt and other related matters. The Arthasastra does-not exempt the woman of herdsman and joint cultivators in matters of debt. Their husbands may be caught for the debt contracted by the wives. Yajnavalkya states that herdsmen, distillers, hunters, etc. should pay back the loan incurred by their wives because they are maintained through their wives.[135] Brhaspati says the same on the ground that the debts were contracted for the affairs of the husbands.[136] Narada explains the reason by saying that the income of these men depends on their wives, and the household expenses have to be defrayed by the wives.[137] Visnu justifies the payment of debt contracted by such wives on the ground that the husbands are supported by their

132. *Ibid.*, 1.18.
133. Kat., 497.
134. Nar., 1.17; Visnu, VI. 29; Yaj., 11.51. 135. Yaj., II.48.
135. *Ibid.*
136. Br., XI.53.
137. Nar., 1.19.

wives.[138] Thus we find here two classes of women in society, and these two classes are being treated differently by the same laws on the same subject matter. It appears that the women of the two upper classes namely the brahmanas and ksatriyas were virtually reduced to the position of domestic servants doing private services and had absolutely nothing to contribute to social production. On the contrary the women belonging to the sudras and vaisyas continued their participation in social production side by side with their menfolk, and as such they did not surrender their economic independence in the way their twice-born counterparts did. "The administration of the household lost its public character, it was no longer the concern of society. It became a private service. The wife became the first domestic servant, pushed out of participation in the social production."[139] Accordingly the smrtis treat the lower class women, due to their participation in production as independent and being capable of the enforcement of civil laws against them. The other class of women who are reduced to the position of domestic servants depend entirely on their husbands and consequently are not considered independent in the eyes of law.

138. Visnu, VI.37.

139. F. Engels, Origin af Family, Private Property and State, Marx and Engels Selected Works, p. 211.

Chapter

12

Rights and Duties in Ancient India

No legal system can subsist without rights and duties and duties in the sense of act and forbearances towards others. The ancient Indian law, like any other legal systems of the ancient world, protected and law recognized the interests of individuals living in the community through lax Rights and duties construed as allowances, benefits and obligations were the part of ancient India legal system. But the concept of tights neither developed into the concept of natural right nor did it nature the psychology which is peculiar to the legal philosophy of the West. Modern concept of right brings with it to the owner of such rights, the sense, that he owns these rights like property. He thinks that others owe him the duty to respect his rights. He is of these rights though such ownership is called only incorporeal ownership. Such rights make men ego-centric. They only fee a concern about themselves with an unconcerned and indifference towards others and the affairs of society. This has resulted in the attitude of man to disown society and become irresponsible to its purposes. The enforcement of one's own legal rights through a legal action, which is just like a battle, is itself steeped in the idea of conflict, and quarrel of civilized combatants. To this extent the lopsided view of one's own rights generates disharmony as well as disintegration of social unity. Thus, the doctrine of natural rights seems to have too much sanctity to the idea of individual rights.

The doctrine of natural tights has its birth in terminological confusion created by natural law doctrine rob son considers that jus Natural produced the doctrine of natural right as a result of the ambiguity of meaning in gerent in the wood 'jus'. One meaning of Jus is right. That which is morally binding. Jus may also be a right, that is, an actual and legally enforceable right. In the latter signification, jus natural means a right of nature, a right possessing inherent validity by virtue of its own essential justice and moral force. It was from this that, the doctrine of natural rights which became the ally of freedom and a weapon of attach against tyranny was evolved.

The doctrine of natural rights has arisen only due to the loosening of control in Western society at the end of the medieval age. Feudalism, a social institution waned and ethics and religion lost hold upon the lives of people and state got so pre-occupied with military expeditions that the affairs of society were neglected while individual was taxed unnecessarily. The individual had to resort to the doctrine of rights for his safeguards against growing despotism of rights for his safeguards against guards against growing despotism of the state. At its initial stage the doctrine of rights performed the social function by giving expression to social purpose expressed by the legal system as a whole. Economics, politics and law all worked both for the individual and the society. There was harmony between the individual ego and the social purpose. Both functions for one another. But the degeneration set in, and process of disorganization started due to the changed circumstances." When this process of degeneration has gone far, as in most European countries it had by the middle of the Eighteenth Century, the indispensable thing is to break the dead organization up and to clear the ground. In the course of doing so, the individual is emancipated and his rights are enlarged; but the idea of social purpose is discredited by the discredit justly obsolete order in which it is embodied."

Due to law economic relations, in the later half of the Seventeenth Century, the state itself began to be considered as a machine. Reformation had already made Church a department of secular Government. Machiavelli asserted the freedom of the state to disown morality and spurn the religious yoke. In the Eighteenth Century, state and Church ceased to work for the maintenance of social ethics and for furtherance of the common ends. Now people began to consider that their economic activity was beyond the jurisdiction of morality, when the medieval democracy was shaken from its roots and democracy of revolution was still in the womb, the Government grew indolent and aristocracy turned irresponsible, Church was now remotely concerned with the daily life of the masses, Christianity lost its great hold, God was reduced into 'frigid' categories of abstractions and individual began to assert his independence and forged the weapon of his rights.

It was said that state had no authority to infringe these rights. The existence of state is only justified in the maintenance of rights. The most important right was that of property. The whole society began to be looked upon as a joint stock company where political power and distribution of goods like dividends were to be determined on the basis of the shares of property. It was though that no moral limitations could be imposed on the economic self-interest of individuals. Rights then appeared as foundations of social order. The pursuit of private end began to be look as public good. French revolutionaries have rights as absolutes of social and political order. Natural law ideology of rights was converted into utilitarian basis by Bentham and his followers. Adam Smith asserted that by economic mechanism these rights could be converted into public good. The individualists, like Turgo, Jefferson, etc. used the doctrine of individual rights to mitigate the abuses of the times, i.e., to do away with the last vestiges of feudalism which was an obstruction to free economic activity in society. Today again due to the failure of *laissez-faire* doctrine and due to class conflicts degeneration of society and commercialization of human relations this doctrine of rights has revealed its destructive visage owing to which curbs have been put on it.

"In England these categories are being bent and twisted till they are no longer recognizable, and well, in time be made harmless. In America where necessity compelled the crystallization of principle in a constitution, they the rigidity of an iron-jacket. The magnificent formulae in which a society of farmers, merchants and master craftsmen enshrined its philosophy of freedom are in danger of becoming fetters used by an Anglo-Saxon business aristocracy to bind insurgent movements of the part of an immigrant and semi-servile proletariat."

There has been a general reaction against the doctrine of natural rights which has become a synonym for exaggerated individualism which is unconcerned with social purpose, and is indifferent to degradation and deprivation of a great mass of humanity. It was castigated as freedom or right to exploit. It was a great obstacle for the legal science because it had extra-legal validity. Austin was of the view that rights are acts or forbearance in the context of positive law. To him the relation of right and duties only prevailed in case of relations between citizens *inter se*. Rights are legal creations sovereign is the creator of rights. Rights against sovereign are contradictions in themselves. Sovereign is the creator of rights. Rights against sovereign are contradictions themselves. Sovereign's power cannot be limited as otherwise it becomes a negation of sovereignty itself. One has no right against the sovereign. Even if it is said that converging has got rights, it is also a negation of sovereignty because rights can only be created by superior authority. No superior authority can be conceived of so as to grant right to the sovereign as this will, in effect, be again the violation of the very logic of sovereignty. No one has superior power to grant rights to the sovereign. Sovereign has then neither rights nor duties. The subjects or citizens have only absolute duties towards the sovereign as he holds the power to command obedience. It is quite clear that against sovereign, which only a personification of state is; the individual can have no rights. The absolute rights are not logically admissible in the science of law as they cannot be explained in the legal relations, apart from the context of law. These rights are only relating to a particular system.

If rights are objective, i.e., if they mean allowances, benefits, etc. allowed by law, one can scarcely object to the doctrine of rights. The advocate of the doctrine of rights want to subordinate the objective law to grant subjective rights as a predetermined *a priori* conditions of civic life. It is pre-supposed, as Kelsen observes:there arise subjective rights and chief among these property, the prototype of all subjective rights, sand only at a later does there emerge the objective law as a political order, protecting and serving the independently arisen subjective right. Accordingly, the whole idea of rights is grounded in the assertion of the subjective right of property. The ideological function of this whole contradictory conception of subjective right is clear enough. It is intended to uphold the idea that subjective rich that is, private property, is, in respect to objective law, a transcendent, *a priori* category in impassable obstacle to the construction of the content of the legal order. This conception of a subjective right different from and independent of the objective law becomes the more important when the latter is recognized to be a constantly changing order, created by and founded neither on nature nor upon the eternal and divine will, particularly when the construction of the objective law proceeds in a democratic fashion. The conception of an independent subjective right, which is even more just than the objective law, is a device to protect the institution of private property from damage at the ideology of subjective right is related to the ethical values if individual freedom and autonomous personality when in this freedom property is always included. Kelsen point out that the concept of right gets undue emphasis in the legal systems of today whereas the concepts of duty gets only step-motherly treatment. A legal system is, no doubt, capable and competent to confer rights on individuals but if it does not so confer them, but only imposes duties, to express legal relations, the system can successfully discharge its legitimate functions. His intention is to put the notion of duty in the forefront. Right is only a device of capitalistic legal order founded upon the concept of property individual interests. In this way, the pure theory of law rejects the dualism of subjective and objective law and thereby has also removed the possibility of any ideological misuse. Legal relationship, called Rights can equally be expressed in terms of duties.

The doctrine of individual right is like wise rejected by Duguit. To him the conception of subjective right is either superfluous or dangerous and he only recognizes duty. According to him here is no such thing as subjective right either in the state or in the individual; the terms social right and individual right are meaningless. As for natural right it was like the general will, an invented by the Eighteen Century merely as a set-off against the pretensions of absolutist of absolutist sovereigns. Duguit, in order to strengthen his view, quotes a passage from Comte, and recommends that it be placed in the Chamber of Deputies.

The word rights deserve to be banished from political terminology as much as the world cause from philosophical terminology. Of these two theological metaphysical concepts, that of right must hence forth be considered immoral and anarchical, that of cause irrational and sophistic Right has no true meaning unless it emanates from a super human will. In its struggle against the cortical authorities, the metaphysics of the five Centuries invented so called human rights which at best could possess only a negative function. At the first attempt to give them a truly organic significance, they immediately betray their anti-social character by striven everlastingly to consecrate individuality. In the state of the actual world which recognizes no celestial prerogative, the idea of right disappears for ever. Every man has duties towards every other man but no man has any rights properly so-called. In other words, the only right which any man can possess is the right, always to do his duty.

According to the Scandinavian realists the net physique of rights is not a blessing for the science of law. Further, the doctrine of rights does not serve the purpose of languet. According to Ross, the notion that between purchase and access to recovery, something like legal right of ownership is created is nonsense. The word "right" has got no semantic reference. It has originated from facts which are not remembered now. The sentences in which it occurs can be rewritten without mentioning it. It only describes the legal relations of factual circumstances which entail legal consequences. The real function of rights is to describe law in force or its application in particular circumstances of the case. The concept of rights does not "designate any phenomenon of any kind that has inserted itself between the conditioning facts and the conditions consequences but is solely a means by which it is possible more or less accurately to visualize the content of a set of legal rules, namely those that concept a certain disjunctive plurality of conditioning facts with a certain cumulative plurality of legal consequences." It appears to this humble author that the concept of right has found entry into different legal systems, only to safeguard the interests of the individual against those who are prone to disown responsibility. In order that life of the society (Social, political, religious, etc.) may remain orderly and peaceful and without conflicts the concept of right was evolved as a device to achieve these goals. Thus is Western when social responsibility was disowned and the individual merely looked to their own interests the doctrine of natural or individual right was formulated. It would thus seen that the doctrine of rights thrives upon distrust and dies in arrogances. It pre-supposes conflicts ridden culture.

It is peculiar effect of Western Culture which has started from Greece where man for the first time, was viewed a political animal. Thus begins a course of journey in conflicts, and antagonism begins, which has not ended as yet. It has its aim in harmony and co-existence but not integration and synthesis.

The great virtue of Indian culture was that it was integrated. Therefore, no protection by way of a doctrine of rights was needed. The State, the individual, and the classes were integrated by the great concept of Dharma conceived as duty which alone was the Right and the individual never thought of having the rights. Law was not the instrument of government or an agent of state nor was it an indifferent spectator to the activities of the individual. Dharma, as a law, was a total concern of Man—a complete philosophy of life and action. Man was only to do duty by which could participate in Dharma right, or Dharma, like Brahman (absolute reality), is metaphysical reality, is immanent and transcendent. Every individual is the embodiment of Brahman when he identifies with it. But when he suffers from limited consciousness and thinks of himself as a limited self, he is divested of Brahmanic consciousness and considers himself separate and apart from the ultimate reality which in fact he is not. In this state of Non-Brahmanic consciousness he lives miserable life. Similarly, Dharma alone is right but when a man thinks of right, he makes himself limited by his selfishness. Brahma as right is objective but then this dharma or right is broken into rights and appropriated by people and institutions for their own interests, the since of right as good or integrating force vanishes. It results into disintegration and disorganization. The only way at own right is to perform one's functions well. Right can only be expressed in being one's duty. Duty is the only passport or title of right. The Gita rightly asks the person to do his/her duty according to dharma which is the law and according to one's station in life (Swadharma). There are no rights but only what one ordinarily means by rights is what others should perform duties for him. Therefore, when one speaks or rights, he is in fact pointing towards the duties at the other side. If duty is the object of the so-called right we need not use the concept of right at all. Brahman, as has been pointed above is the metaphysical reality which is unknowable in its unmanifested form. But when it is manifested through lila or 'kama' it becomes Sakriya Brahman. It is expressed in religion as Sugan Brahman or God. Its social aspect which is also the legal aspect is dharma. Which, in metaphysical aspect, is the character, function and nature of the world, the mystic force, the quality or property of all things. In order to reach Brahman one must has true knowledge. In order to reach Dharma one must have true deed or faithful performance of one's own duty. Detachment another name of tolerance and co-operation is a *sine qua non* both for knowledge of Reality (Brahman) and enforcement of right or Dharma. For the former, one has to de-personalize in knowledge, and for the latter, in action. Indian ethics, Metaphysics and jurisprudence are then variations of the same theme through different media. In the West the juristic, Summon Bonun is reached approximately through the doctrines of natural rights, common law, public policy, equity, justice, etc. but due to their limited approaches the reach to juristic heaven is inaccessible to them. The concept of dharma includes all the western legal ideology shorn off their antagonisms.

The doctrine of rights did not get the fruitful soil in India. In Indian Language there is no appropriate word do nothing only right. The word "Adhikar's has not the meaning of rights in Sanskrit. It is only due to the western influence that it has taken over the meaning or right which was necessary for the movement of freedom against British regimes. Adhikari in Sanskrit is one who is fit or able or qualified for a particular task. He is not understood in the sense of a person owning power or rights. The ancient Indian is not allowed to speak as owner of the rights but he is a participant in the right. He is not in any danger of alienation of himself society. He is not an anarchist, who distrusts state and government. To him the state is not a confiscator of right but a follower of right. To him religion is not an institutionalized violence against other religions. Society to him is not something like a prison where there are checks or restraints on him. He never considers his civilization as a curse. The Ancient Indian lives and thinks in freshness of spirit, works for synthesis and integration through his thought and action.

The inappropriateness of the doctrine of rights is again proved by modern Indian case law and consequent amendment of the constitution several times which is nothing else but the revival of the concept of dharma which puts duty on the forefront. No amount of amendment, no modification, no further borrowing form alien soils will remedy the gaps that are until and unless were revert (making such allowances for new changes due to science and technology) to his basic Indian concept of law which is already therein in ancient concept of 'Dharma'.

Chapter

13

Judicial and Administrative System in Mughal Period

Mughal period started with the advent of Muslim Rulers after the decay of Hindu Kingdom through various invasion by Mongols, Afgans and other foreign invaders. The powerful among Muslim rulers were Mughals. They started their position in good position. They were raised up to good height roughly throughout India before the Mughal period the ancient legal principles, as shown by me in the book were applicable, but the Mughal rulers substituted their own system throughout India irrespective of any caste, creed and religion except in some specific matters.

Judicial and administrative system during Mughal empires was matchless, excellent and complete in all senses. Let us have a brief perusal of Mughal system as a whole.

Though the Mughal Emperors had absolute powers, they appointed a number of officers in the different departments of the Government for the transaction of its multitudinous affairs. The chief departments of the State were: (a) the Imperial House-hold under the Khan-i-Saman, (b) the Exchequer under Deccan, (c) the Military Pay and Accounts Office under the Mir Bakhshi, (d) the Judiciary under the Chief Qazi, (e) Religious Endowments and charities under the Chief Sadr or Sadr-us-Sudur, and (f) the Censorship of Public Morals under the Mohtasib. The Diwan or Wazir was usually the highest officer in the State, being sole incharge of revenues and finance. The Bakhshi discharged a variety of functions. While he was the pay-master-General of all the officers of the State, who "theoretically belonged to the military department", he was also responsible for the recruiting of the army, and for maintaining lists of mansabdars and other high officials; and when preparing for a battle he has a complete muster-roll of the army before the Emperor. The Khan-i-Saman or the Lord High Steward had charge of the whole imperial household "in reference to both great and small things." The Muhtamibs or Censors of Public Morals looked after the enforcement of the prophet's commands and the laws of morality. The other officers, somewhat inferior in status to those mentioned above, were the Mir Atish or Daroga-i-Topkhana (head of the artillery), the Daroga of Dak Chowki (head of the correspondence department).

The Daroga of the Mint, the Mir Mal or the Lord Privy Seal, the Mustayfi or the Auditor-General, the Nazir-i-Buyulat or the Superintendent of the Imperial Workshop, the Mushriff or the Revenue Secretary, the Mir Bahri or the Lord of the Admiralty, the Mir Barr or the Superintendent of Forests, the Waqa-i-navis or News Reporters, the Mir Arz or the officer-in-charge of petitions presented to the Emperor, the Mir Manzil or the Quarter-master-General, and the Mir Tezak or the Master of Ceremonies. We shall discuss first police, then, Judicial Land Revenue System.

(I) THE POLICE

So far as the rural areas were concerned, the Mughuls introduced no new arrangements for. the prevention and detection of crimes. These remained, as from time immemorial, under the head-man of the village and his subordinate watchmen. The system which afforded a fair degree of security in the local areas with only occasional disturbances in times of disorder, survived till the beginning of the nineteenth century. In the cities and towns, all police duties including the task of maintaining public order and decency, were entrusted to the Kotwals, whose duties, as enumerated in the Ain-i-Akbari, were multifarious (i) to detect thieves, (ii) to regulate prices and check weights and measures, (iii) to keep watch at night and patrol the city, (iv) to keep up registers of houses, frequented roads, and of citizens and watch the movements of strangers, (v) to employ spies from among the vagabonds, gather information about the affairs of the neighbouring villages and the income and expenditure of the various classes of people, (vi) to prepare an inventory of, and take charge of, the property of deceased or missing persons who left no heirs, (vii) to prevent the slaughter of oxen, buffalos, horses or camels, and (viii) to prevent the burning of women against their will, and circumcision below the age of twelve, Sir J.N. Sarkar believes that this long list of the Kotwals' duties in the Ain represents "only the ideal for the Kotwali" and not "the actual State of things. But Manucci gives from personal observation an exhaustive account of the Kotwalis duties. It is, however, certain that the Kotwali's main business was to preserve peace and public security in the urban areas. In the districts or Sarkars, law and order were maintained usually by officers like the Faujddrs." The Taujddr, as his name suggests, was only the commander of a military force stationed in the country. He had to put down smaller rebellions, disperse or arrest robber gangs, take cognizance of all violent crimes, and make demonstrations of force to overawe, opposition to the revenue authorities, or the criminal judge, or the censor." The police arrangements were in some respects effective, though "the State of public security varied greatly from place to place and from time to time.

(2) JUDICIAL SYSTEM

Nothing like modern legislation, or a written code of laws, existed in the Mughul period. The only notable exceptions to this were the twelve ordinances of Jahangir and the Fatawa-i-Alamgiri, a digest of Muslim law prepared

Moreland, India as the Death of Akbar, p. 66ft.

under Aurangzeb's supervision. The judges chiefly followed the Quranic injunctions or percepts, the Fatawas or previous interpretations of the Holy Law by eminent jurists and the qanunus or ordinances of the Emperors. They did not ordinarily disregard customary laws and sometimes followed principles of equity. Above all, the Emperor's interpretation prevailed, provided they did not run counter to the sacred laws.

The Mughul Emperors regarded speedy administration of justice as one of their important duties, and their officers did not enjoy any special protection in this respect under anything like Administrative Law. "If I were guilty of an unjust act," said Akbar, "I would rise in judgment against myself." Peruschi, writes on the authority of Monserrate that "as to the administration of justice he is most zealous and watchful." The love of justice of the other Emperors like Jahangir, Shah Jahan and Aurangzeb, has been testified to by some contemporary European travellers. Though approach to the Emperor through all kinds of official obstructions was not very easy, at least two Mughul Emperors, Akbar and Jahangir, granted to their subjects the right of direct petitioning (which was only won in England after a hard fight). The latter allowed a chain with bells to be hung outside his palace to enable petitioners to bring their grievances to the notice of the Emperor.

The Qazi-ul-Qazat or the Chief Qazi was the principle judicial officer in the realm. He appointed Qazis in every provincial capital. The Qazis made investigations into, and tried civil as well as criminal cases of both the Hindus and the Muslims; the Muftis expounded Muslim Law and the Mir Adls drew up and 'pronounced judgments'. The Qazis were expected to be "Just, honest, impartial, to hold trails in the presence of the parties and at the Court-house and the seat of government, not to accept presents from the people where they served, nor to attend entertainments given to anybody and everybody, and they were. asked to know poverty to be their glory." But in practice they abused their authority and as Sir J.N. Sarkar observes; "the Qazi's department became a byword and reproach in Mughul times." There were no primary courts below those of the Qazis and the villagers and the inhabitants of smaller towns, having no Qazis over them, settled their differences locally "by appeal to the caste courts or panchayats, the arbitration of an impartial umpire (Salis), or by a resort to force." The Sadr-us-Sudur or the Chief Sadr exercised supervision over the lands granted by the Emperors or prices to pious men, scholars and monks, and tried cases relating to these. Below him there was a local Sadr in every province.

Above the urban and provincial courts was the Emperor himself, who, as the "Khalif of the age", was the fountain of justice and the final court of appeal. Sometimes he acted as Court of first instance too. Fines could be imposed and severe punishments, like amputation, mutilation and whipping, could be inflicted by the Courts without any reference to the Emperor, but his consent was necessary in inflicting capital punishment. There was no regular jail system, but the prisoners were confined in forts.

(3) THE REVENUE SYSTEM

The revenues of the Mughul Empire may be grouped under the heads—central or imperial and local or provincial. The local revenue, which was apparently collected and spent without reference to the finance authorities of the central government was derived from various minor duties and taxes levied on "production and consumption, on trades and occupations, on various incidents of social life, and most of all on transport." The major sources of central revenue were land revenue, customs, mint, inheritance, plunder and indemnities, presents, monopolies and the poll-tax. Of these, land revenue formed, as in old days, the most important source of the State income.

The important revenue experiments of the surs were undone in the period of confusion and disorders following the reign of Sher Shah and Islam Shah. But the old machinery of government and the time-honoured and procedures, 'must have been inherited by Akbar', who found at his accession three kinds of land in the country—the Khalsa or crown-lands, the Jagir lands, enjoyed by some nobles who collected the local revenues out of which they sent a portion to the central exchequer and kept the rest for themselves and the Sayurghal lands, granted on free tenure. After securing his freedom from the influence of Bairam and that of the ladies of the harem, Akbar realised the importance of reorganising the finances of his growing empire, which were in a hopelessly confused state. Thus in 1570-71, Muzaffar Khan Turbati, assisted by Raja Todar Mall, prepared a revised assessment of the land revenue, "based on estimates framed by the local Qanungoes and checked by ten superior Qanungoes at headquarters." After Gujarat had been conquered. Todar Mall effected there a regular survey of the land, and the assessment was made "with reference to the area and quality of the land." In 1575-76 Akbar made a new and disastrous experiment by abolishing the old revenue areas and dividing whole of the Empire, with the exception of the provinces of Gujarat, Bengal and Bihar, into a large number of units, each yielding one kror (crore) a year, and laced over each of them an officer called the Krori, whose duties were to collect revenues and encourage. cultivation. But the Kroris soon grew corrupt and their tyranny reduced the peasants to great misery. Their offices were, therefore abolished and the revenue divisions were restored, though the title of Krori continued to survive at least till the reign of Shah Jahan.

Important revenue reforms were introduced in 1582, when Todar Mall was appointed the Diwan-i-Ashraf. Hitherto were fixed annually on the basis of production and statistics of current prices, and the demands of the State thus varied from year to year. Todar Mall established a standard or "regulation" system of revenue, collection, the chief features of which were (i) survey of land, (ii) classification of land, (iii) fixation of rates. Lands were carefully surveyed, and for measurement the old units, whose length fluctuated with the change of season, were replaced by the Ilahi Gaz or yard, which was equal to about thirty three inches, tanab or tent-rope, and jarib of bamboos joined by iron rings, which assured a constant measure. Land was classification into four classes according to "the continuity or discontinuity of cultivation": (i) Polaj or land capable of being annually cultivated, (ii) Parauti or land kept fallow for some time to recover productive capacity, (iii) Chauhar or land that had lain fallow for three or four years, and (iv) Banjar or land uncultivated for five years or longer. Only the area actually cultivated was assessed, said, in order to ascertain the average produce of land belonging to each class, the mean of the three grades into which it was divided was taken into consideration. The demand of the State was fixed at one-third of the actual produce, which the ryots could pay either in cash or in kind. The cash rates varied according to crops. This revenue system, as applied to Northern India, Gujarat, and with some modifications, to the Deccan, was rayalwad that is, "the actual cultivators of the soil were the persons responsible for the annual payment of the fixed revenue." In the outlying portions of the Empire, this system was not applied, but each of these was dealt with as local circumstances required.

For purposes of administration and revenue collection, the Empire was divided into Subahs, which again were subdivided into sarkars, each of which in turn comprised a number of parganas. Each parasana was a union of several villages. The amalguzar or revenue collector incharge of a district was assisted by a large subordinate staff. Apart from the village Muqaddam (headman) and the village patwari, who were servants of the village community and not of the State, there were measures and karkuns who prepared the seasonal crop statistics; the Qanungo, who kept records of the revenue payable by the villages; the Bitikcha or accountant; and the Potdar or district treasurer. These officers were instructed to collect revenue with due care and caution and "not to extend the hand of demand out of season." The Emperors were for ever "issuing orders to their officers to show leniency and. consideration to the peasants in collecting tie revenue, to give up all abwabs and to relieve local distress." There are instances in the reigns of Shah Jahan and Aurangzeb of extortionate revenue officials and even provincial governors being dismissed on complaints being made against them by the subjects to the Emperors. Though the lower revenue officers, especially those in the outlying provinces and districts, were not above corruption and malpractices, "the highest, were on the whole, just and statesman like" with few exceptions.

The success or failure of the revenue system thus organised must have depended on the quality and nature of the administration at the centre, and evils could not but appear when administrative machinery was getting out of gear in Aurangzeb's reign. But on the whole it principles were sound and "the practical instructions to the officials all that could be desired." The ryots got certain amount of security and the fluctuations of the State revenue were prevented, or at least minimised. Further, the ryots were not evicted from their holdings for default of payment, and the "custom of payment by the division of the crop", on the basis of the actual produce of a year, was better than the modern money rent system by which one has to pay the fixed amount irrespective of the harvest of the year. The demand at the ratio of one-third, though rather high, as compared with one-sixth prescribed by Hindu law and custom or with what a modern landowner gets, was not a heavy burden on the peasants, were compensated, by the State with the abolition or remission of various cesses and taxes.

Above analysis, has shown that the entire judicial, administrative and revenue systems during the Mughul Empire, was unscientific, uncodified and some how it was a face saving device to the king emperors. Those, who were very close to the Emperors or whose approach to the palace was easy and assessable, administration and justice, was balanced and truth speaking. Obviously, those who were residents of cities and towns always obtained benefit and asked for justice and maintained the balance of administration but those who were residents of villages or those who were residents at a distance from the imperial palaces, they always suffered, they · never obtained relief. Their thirst for justice and their tears from the eyes against the grievances were never wiped out. They always kept mum for their grievances. Certainly, it was a fact that when any irregularity or injustice came to the knowledge of the emperor that was always remedied without any kind of discrimination with the Society. But this is a fact that Emperor always tried to dispense justice and to keep strict discipline in the administration, as far as possible by him, particularly the names of the Akbar and Jahangir cannot be forgotten in this respect.

Chapter

14

Conclusion and Future Prospects

We have examined so far in the present book pre-British India and pre-Independence era of judicial and administrative working of our India. It is, no doubt, true that our nation is not only highly civilized but its culture was also highly advanced. Everyone in the world followed us in ancient period, then there was change in the position. Our deterioration of culture started and we lost gradually our glory of culture and system. Lastly we were compelled to live under foreign system which was imposed on us by our invader rulers, who gradually picked up the entire nation in their own command. We deviated our own path and culture. Dilution started in our system and gradually our original system was confined only to books. The customs and conventions of invader rulers were also adopted by us, and lastly in the lack of cosmopolitan rule (mixture of our and foreign ruler) was available or purely the system of foreign ruler was enforced.

Today, we are looking that even after more than 50 years of independence we have not yet traced out our own original system or path of society. We are still banking roughly upon British rulers made laws in all respect. Still the judicial, administrative, military and even governmental system is still based on British pattern. Now we want to know how long it shall last, upto what time we shall be governed by these rulers which have been made by the foreigners. We should awake up with fresh zeal and courage to change the foreign system. We should make laws for the governance of country looking into our culture, system and nation, which are best suited to us. We should see Swami Vivekanand has shown new path to world in philosophy. The world cannot forget the contribution of Dr. Radhakrishnan and Rajendra Prasad. We should further create other landmarks also to show to the world. We have the capacity to be governed by our own system which is one of the oldest in the world. We may modify that, amend that as per convenience as to keep pace in society so that we may also remain up-to-date and up-to-time. Our system is still the best but we have to get it corrected as and when required looking into time, place and circumstances. Further, we should not hesitate to adopt any thing, any concept which is good to ourselves. We know that our culture and system is highly broad minded. We know to adjust with everyone. Let our goal should be to raise our own system with necessary changes to show to the world that we are not completely independent. Let us see what happen in future. We have to wait for it with anxiety.

Index